THE LITTLE BOOK OF
CELTIC

A CELTIC A to Z

Written by Graham Betts

THE LITTLE BOOK OF
CELTIC

This edition first published in the UK in 2007
By Green Umbrella

© Green Umbrella Publishing 2007

www.greenumbrella.co.uk

Publishers Jules Gammond, Vanessa Gardner

Printed and bound in Poland

ISBN 13 978-1-905009-88-6

Contents

Aitken

BORN IN IRVINE ON 24 NOVEMBER 1958 Roy Aitken could have pursued a career as a pianist having attained university grades whilst still at secondary school but chose instead to become a footballer. Initially signed by Celtic Boys Club he joined the Parkhead outfit in 1972 with his first team debut three years later, in a League Cup tie against Stenhousemuir in September 1975, and Roy was to finish the season with a total of 16 appearances to his name.

By the following season, 1976-77, Roy was established as a first team regular at the heart of the defence despite being still a teenager, operating at centre-half but with the freedom to move forward as and when the opportunity arose. This proved the launch pad for a double success, with the League title being won in a canter ahead of Rangers and the same opposition being seen off in the Scottish Cup. Only the League Cup

FAR LEFT
Roy Aitken, 1987

LEFT Roy Aitken holds up the trophy after the Scottish Cup Final match against Rangers, 1989

from the League and Scottish Cup, with six League titles and five Cup wins being his reward. He also proved his worth on the international stage, winning 57 caps for Scotland, of which 50 were won whilst on the books of Celtic, as well as 16 caps for Scotland at Under-21 level.

Roy was to make a total of 672 appearances for the Celtic first team, netting 53 goals, with all three of his managers – Jock Stein, Billy McNeill (twice) and David Hay – relying on Roy to provide leadership and inspiration on the field. None could say they were ever left disappointed as Roy galvanised those around him to greater effort. He was surprisingly allowed to leave to join Newcastle United in January 1990 and Celtic struggled to find a player with similar passion for a number of years. Roy meanwhile went on to make 54 appearances for the Magpies before returning to Scotland to play for St Mirren where he finished his playing career. A brief spell in management with Aberdeen was not entirely successful, prompting Roy to turn to coaching. He enjoyed considerable success at Leeds United under David O'Leary before linking up again with O'Leary at Aston Villa.

eluded Celtic that term, beaten in the Final by Aberdeen. Indeed, the League Cup was to prove something of an elusive trophy for Roy, with only one winners' medal collected during his time with the club. There was more than adequate compensation to be gained

Attendances

THESE FIGURES ARE CELTIC'S BEST
attendances at Celtic Park in each of the
major competitions.

Scottish League v Rangers,
(1/1/1938) – 92,000

Scottish FA Cup v Hearts,
(22/2/1939) – 80,840

Scottish League Cup v Rangers,
(13/8/1949) – 70,000

Europe v Liverpool,
14/4/1966) – 80,000*

*Celtic v Leeds United on 15/4/1970
attracted a crowd of 136,505 but this
was played at Hampden Park.

Auld

AS A MEMBER OF THE SUCCESSFUL European Cup winning side of 1967 Bertie Auld is assured his place in the Celtic Hall of Fame, but he could so easily have missed out on the greatest of all club honours. Born in Glasgow on 23 April 1938 he was spotted by Celtic whilst playing for Maryhill Harp and signed for the club in 1955. Handed a debut against Partick Thistle in February 1959 Bertie made sure he stamped his authority on both the match and the club right from the start of his career, actions that ensured he was considered a thorn in the side by opponents and even one or two within Celtic Park.

It was Celtic chairman Robert Kelly who virtually insisted that Bertie be sold after too many on the field indiscretions and he was transferred to Birmingham City in May 1961, just in time to play in the Final of the Inter Cities Fairs Cup against Roma which the Italian side duly won. Whilst Bertie's heart was still at Celtic Park his time at St Andrews was not without its highlights, including a winners' medal from the Football League Cup after victory over local rivals Aston Villa. As far as Bertie was concerned, however, the only local rivals he wanted to do battle with were Rangers and in January 1965 he jumped at the chance to return to Celtic, especially when it was rumoured that former Celtic player Jock Stein could be returning to Celtic Park to take over as manager. With hindsight, it may even have been Jock Stein who initiated Bertie's return.

Jock duly arrived two months after Bertie and switched the former errant left-winger to midfield, taught him to control his aggression and reaped the benefits when Bertie formed a particularly effective partnership with Bobby Murdoch. With Bertie and Bobby bossing things in the middle, Celtic were not a side that could be pushed off the ball, and this duo was to win a host of honours with the club. By the time Bertie left Celtic Park again in 1971 it was with seven League Championship medals, six Scottish Cup medals, six League Cup medals and, most impressive of all, a winners' medal from the European Cup.

Despite this domestic success Bertie was only honoured three times by his

country, even though he performed the same kind of role for which later hard men such as Graeme Souness earned countless caps. Under-appreciated at international level he may have been, but never at Celtic Park. Bertie left the club in 1971 and joined Hibernian on a free transfer where he finished his playing career. He then had spells in management with Partick Thistle, Hibernian and Dumbarton before effectively leaving the game, although he can still be seen on Celtic TV where he has developed a reputation for saying what he thinks, irrespective of who he upsets, just as he did as a player.

Bonner

PAT BONNER SPENT SOME seventeen years guarding the Celtic goal but is perhaps better known by football fans for his accomplishments for the Republic of Ireland. Born in Clochglas in County Donegal on 24 May 1960, he joined Celtic as an eighteen-year-old and made his debut in the 2-1 win over Motherwell on 17 March 1979. He was to make two appearances that season but did not become a regular until the 1980-81 season when he eventually displaced Peter Latchford and provided Celtic with a settled and competent goalkeeper, something they had lacked for some considerable time.

During the course of the next fifteen seasons, Pat was to play his part in delivering four League titles, three Scottish Cups and the League Cup once, with Pat gaining a reputation for being a formidable shot stopper and brave beyond the call of duty in throwing himself at the feet of onrushing opponents.

First capped for the Republic of Ireland against Poland, Pat would go on to make eighty appearances for his country, making him Celtic's most capped player. His last cap came in 1996 and in between times he appeared in two World Cup campaigns, including the glorious Irish march to the quarter-finals in 1990. Indeed, it was Pat's superb penalty shoot out save from Daniel Timofte that ensured the Republic of Ireland beat Romania in the second round.

His final appearance for Celtic came in the Scottish Cup Final of 1995, after which he retired. Pat linked up with the Republic of Ireland again under Brian Kerr, becoming technical director and goalkeeping coach in 2003, although when Kerr's contract was not renewed, Pat left his position following the arrival of new head coach Steve Staunton. He then became a television presenter with TV3 Ireland.

BELOW Pat Bonner directs his team mates during a match against Aberdeen

Burns

WHILST HIS TIME AT CELTIC PARK as a manager did not deliver the success that was expected, Tommy Burns' reputation within the club has not been tarnished by the experience – he is still appreciated as a Celtic man through and through.

Born in Glasgow on 16 December 1956, Tommy joined Celtic from Maryhill Juniors in 1973 and had to wait two years before making his League debut for the club, which came in a 2-1 home defeat to Dundee in April 1975. At the time manager Jock Stein was rebuilding the side after the nine-in-a-row glories and would eventually utilise Tommy as the midfield anchor, although it was not until the 1980-81 season that Tommy could claim to be a regular in the side.

He would eventually go on to help the club win six League Championships, the Scottish Cup four times and the League Cup once, as well as earning eight caps for Scotland. For all his domestic success, it was the impact he had on the games in European competition that most caught the eye, with many rival managers claiming Tommy to be the heartbeat of the Celtic side. None other than Johan Cruyff, who played for Ajax against them in the European Cup in 1982, claimed him to have been the best Celtic player on the park in their encounters.

Tommy made 357 League appearances and a total of 508 appearances in all competitions for Celtic, scoring 82 goals before moving on to Kilmarnock in 1989 where he finished his playing career. He was appointed manager at Rugby Park in 1992 and took them to the First Division title and with it promotion into the Premier League in 1992-93.

After one season in the top flight with Kilmarnock, which saw them in relative safety in mid-table, Tommy accepted the call from Celtic Park to take over both a side and club in some considerable turmoil. With lack of success on the field from previous managers Liam Brady and Lou Macari, expensive re-development of the stadium and a recently completed boardroom takeover, Tommy had stepped into a lions' den. Things did not start well either,

with supporters not exactly taking to playing home matches at Hampden Park whilst Celtic Park was being developed, and a surprising defeat in the League Cup Final against First Division outfit Raith Rovers on penalties. Whilst the League proved to be well beyond Celtic (they were ultimately to finish fourth behind Rangers, Motherwell and Hibernian) progress was made in the Scottish Cup, with Celtic ultimately proving successful with a 1-0 win over Airdrie, their first trophy win of any kind in six years.

That was to be the only trophy delivered during Tommy Burns' time as manager of the club, his contract not being renewed when it expired in 1997 and he later had a spell managing Reading in England. Tommy returned to Scotland to become assistant manager of the national side under Bertie Vogts and retained the position when Walter Smith took over. He also returned to Celtic Park in 2005 as part of the team assembled by Gordon Strachan.

LEFT Tommy Burns in action during the 1988 Scottish Cup Final against Dundee

Celtic Park

ALTHOUGH IT IS MORE POPULARLY known as Parkhead, Celtic's ground is officially called Celtic Park, Parkhead being the area of Glasgow that has been home to the club for more than one hundred years.

Almost unique among football clubs, Celtic began building a stadium before they assembled a team, with large numbers of the East End of Glasgow's Irish immigrants helping create the first Celtic Park on land that was rented for £50 per annum. This was officially opened with a visit from Rangers on 28 May 1888 (the ground had already staged a match between Hibernian and Cowlairs on 8 May 1888), with Rangers' side being a mixture of established first team players, a number of reserves and one or two guests. Since it was Celtic's first match, their side was composed almost entirely of guest players, predominantly from the Hibernian club, and Neil McCallum earned the distinction of scoring the first goal at Celtic Park in a match Celtic were ultimately to win 5-2 in front of 2,000 spectators who paid sixpence each for the privilege.

The almost immediate success of Celtic, who reached the Final of the Scottish Cup the following season, saw attendances increase at the stadium, with 8,000 being present for the 8-0 Cup win over Cowlairs. The following season Celtic were drawn against the leading club side of the day, Queen's Park, and 26,000 crammed into Celtic Park to witness a goalless draw. Although Celtic were beaten in the replay and faced nothing more than friendly fixtures for the rest of the season, the Scottish League was formed in 1890 and Celtic were to be founder members, thus guaranteeing regular fixtures and thus income for the future.

Celtic's success in getting vast numbers of spectators through the doors (the 26,000 crowd for the visit of Queen's Park was then a record crowd for a football fixture in Scotland) prompted the landlord of Celtic Park to announce a steep increase in rent for

1892, from £50 per annum to £450. Rather than give in to such demands Celtic looked elsewhere for a new ground and found a plot of land 200 yards away, a quarry alongside Janefield Street.

Whilst much of the work was once again performed by volunteer Irishmen, more professional help was at hand for the actual design of the stadium. The new ground could hold 70,000 people and featured a stand in the northern part of the ground that could accommodate 3,500. The ground was completed with a smart pavilion in

which were housed the changing rooms and offices. It was at this point that the ground acquired another of its nicknames – one local was heard to describe Celtic Park as 'like leaving the graveyard to enter Paradise', and Paradise is another name that has been associated with Celtic Park ever since.

Whilst Celtic had been formed as something of a charitable institution, the club's success on the field had funded development off it and in 1897 the club became a limited company. Almost immediately came further developments at Celtic Park –

CELTIC PARK

the lease for the land was purchased at the then considerable sum of £10,000 and club director James Grant built an impressive glass fronted stand on the south side of the stadium. In a unique move, Grant was given permission by the club to run the stand as his own private business, charging a premium to those who wished to view their football with considerably more comfort than those standing on the terraces. Although the Grant Stand was luxurious (according to one advertisement it offered 'freedom from atmospheric inconvenience') the project was a disaster, since condensation steamed up the windows and those inside couldn't see what was happening outside!

A fire in 1904 destroyed the Pavilion and Main Stand (it was suspected to have been arsonists) and the Grant Stand had to be renovated to become the only seated stand within the ground. A new Pavilion was built, but this accommodated standing spectators only. A quarter of a century later Celtic set about renovating the stadium once more, with the Grant Stand being demolished to make way for a new South Stand. As it was being demolished, fire broke out in the Pavilion opposite and this was completely destroyed within an hour!

By the time the 'new' ground was rebuilt, it was claimed that it could accommodate more than 90,000 fans and it was reported that 92,000 packed in for the traditional New Year's Day match against Rangers, but in fact the attendance was nearer 83,000.

1990s presented the club with one of two options: converting shallow terracing into seating and drastically reduce the capacity, or virtually start again. Although trailing their Glasgow rivals Rangers on the field, the decision was taken to completely renovate the ground, which required a temporary move to Hampden Park whilst Celtic Park was being refurbished. The resulting ground, with the stands completely enveloping the pitch, is the second biggest club ground in Britain (only Manchester United's Old Trafford is bigger) with room for 60,000. Three sides of the ground feature a double tiered stand and the lower Main Stand houses the club's museum.

Celtic Park today is a magnificent ground, full to the brim every other week as Celtic enjoy renewed success on the field. When Hampden Park was itself being renovated, Celtic Park took over hosting a number of major Cup Finals and Internationals. Although Hampden Park is open once again, Celtic Park will once again host a Scotland international in 2006 – Robbie Williams has Hampden Park booked when Scotland kick off their 2008 European Championship campaign!

The fifty year period after the Second World War saw new stands, new roofs, floodlighting and a host of other developments, but there did not seem to be any central planning and Celtic Park was a mixture of old and new, standing and seating and places covered and uncovered and open to the elements. The Taylor Report, which required the ground to go all-seating by the early

Chalmers

STEVIE CHALMERS SCORED THE most important goal in Celtic's history, the winner in the European Cup Final in 1967, yet midway through the season was seemingly on his way out of the club as Jock Stein looked to reshuffle his attacking options and bought Willie Wallace with the intention of partnering him with Joe McBride. An injury to McBride gave Stevie a reprieve, one that both he and Celtic made the most of.

Stevie was almost lost to professional football, for as a youngster he suffered from a series of illnesses, all of which convinced those clubs that watched him play for Ashfield Juniors that he would never make it in the professional game. Eventually Celtic manager Jimmy McGrory gave him a chance and he made his debut, at the age of 22, against Airdrie on 10 March 1959. Although it was to take some time before the glory days returned to Celtic Park, Stevie made an instant impact on the side, finishing top goalscorer in 1960-61 with 26 goals (20 in the League, five in the Scottish Cup and one in the League Cup).

Unfortunately no one else in the side managed double figures in the League and Celtic languished in fourth place.

Stevie topped the charts again in 1963-64 with 28 League goals and ten in other competitions, but Celtic could only improve up to third place, a temporary improvement as they slipped down the table to eighth the following term, McGrory's last as Celtic manager. Stevie had knocked in twelve League goals and fourteen in other competitions to finish top goalscorer again and with the arrival of Joe McBride from Motherwell was expected to share the goalscoring responsibilities.

Joe and Stevie grabbed 63 goals between them in the 1965-66 season, Jock Stein's first, with Bobbie Lennox and John Hughes contributing a further 47 as Celtic won the League title and League Cup, finished runners-up in the Scottish Cup and reached the semi-finals of the European Cup Winners' Cup. By then Stevie was almost 30 years of age and Jock swooped for Willie Wallace of Hearts as a new partner for Joe McBride in December 1966, but an injury sustained by Joe forced something of a rethink, with Stevie linking up with Willie in the record-breaking 1966-67 season. Stevie finished top goalscorer, hitting 36 goals, but none was as vital as the winner against Internazionale in the European Cup Final.

Although that was the last season Stevie Chalmers topped the Celtic goalscoring charts, he remained with the club until 1971, by which time he had made 406 appearances and hit 219 goals, with his 147 in the League enough to earn him fifth place in the overall list. Stevie moved on to Morton when his Celtic career came to an end but would return to the club as a coach when he retired from playing.

Clark

RIGHT John Clark
running on to the pitch

JIMMY JOHNSTONE GAVE THE side flair, Bobby Murdoch was the midfield prompter, Tommy Gemmell and Stevie Chalmers scored the goals and Billy McNeill collected the trophy, but one of the most important members of Celtic's European Cup winning side of 1967 was John Clark, who along with Tommy Gemmell appeared in every one of Celtic's matches in 1966-67.

Something of an unsung hero, John was born in Larkhall on 13 March 1941 and joined Celtic from Larkhall Thistle in 1958. He made his debut during the 1959-60 season but did not get to hold down a regular place until the 1963-64 season, although he was a virtual ever-present after Jock Stein became manager.

By the time he left for Morton in 1971 he had made 163 League appearances (and scored just one goal!) and a total of 284 first team appearances, netting three goals. He had helped the club win six League titles, four Scottish Cups and Five League Cups as well as the European Cup in 1967, although he did not appear in the 1970 losing side.

When his playing career came to an end he returned to Celtic and is currently employed as kitman.

Collins

KNOWN AS 'THE WEE BARRA' ON account of his diminutive size (he was just 5' 4" tall), Bobby Collins more than made up for his lack of inches with his will to win and never say die attitude, traits that were extremely beneficial to Celtic during the topsy turvy 1950s.

Born in Govanhill on 16 February 1931, Bobby joined Celtic from Pollok Juniors after a brief spell with Everton and made his debut in the League Cup clash with Rangers in August 1949, a veritable baptism of fire. He more than made his presence felt, helping Celtic to a 3-2 win with a stirring performance on the wing, although by the following season he was switched to inside-right. There he made the most of a thunderbolt shot and would go on to plunder 117 goals for Celtic, of which 80 were scored in the League. He also helped the club win one League title and two League Cups and would go on to collect 22 caps for Scotland.

Whilst his enthusiastic style was popular among the fans and his teammates, others within Celtic Park were not so enamoured and after a strong challenge on the Clyde goalkeeper in the 1955 Scottish Cup Final, chairman Robert Kelly instructed manager Jimmy McGrory not to select Collins for the replay – Celtic went down after a lacklustre performance 1-0.

In 1958 he was sold to Everton for £39,000, overcoming the homesickness that had blighted his original sojourn at Goodison. He was not the same player at Everton that he had been at Celtic, and Celtic missed his inspiration after his departure, although Bobby resurrected his career with Leeds United enough to be named Footballer of the Year in 1965 and Celtic eventually found players who were just as desperate to win. Bobby later played for Bury and Oldham before moving on to management with Hull City, Huddersfield Town and Barnsley and coaching at Blackpool.

BELOW Bobby Collins

Craig

JIM CRAIG WAS BORN IN Glasgow on 30 April 1943 and was spotted by Celtic whilst playing for Glasgow University, signing for the club in 1963. The arrival of Jock Stein as manager saw him elevated to become the regular right-back, helping Celtic win the League title in 1966, their first title success in twelve years.

The following season was to bring even greater honours with a clean sweep of League, League Cup, Scottish Cup and European Cup. Whilst Jim was normally a reliable and confident full-back, it was he who made an uncharacteristic mistake in the European Cup Final against Internazionale, being under pressure and fouling Cappellini after seven minutes inside the penalty area. Inter scored from the resulting penalty, but Jim recovered his composure and Celtic never panicked as they eventually clawed their way back into the match.

Although Jim remained at Celtic Park until 1972 and helped the club win seven League titles, he was not a member of the side that returned to the European Cup Final in 1970. The following season he had the misfortune to score an own goal against Rangers in the Scottish Cup Final but Celtic managed to overcome the set-back and win the trophy with a 2-1 victory. The following year he collected another winners' medal in what was his final game for Celtic as Hibernian were beaten 6-1, as good a way to bow out as any. Jim then played briefly for Hellenic and Sheffield Wednesday but made only seven appearances for the Hillsborough club before finally retiring.

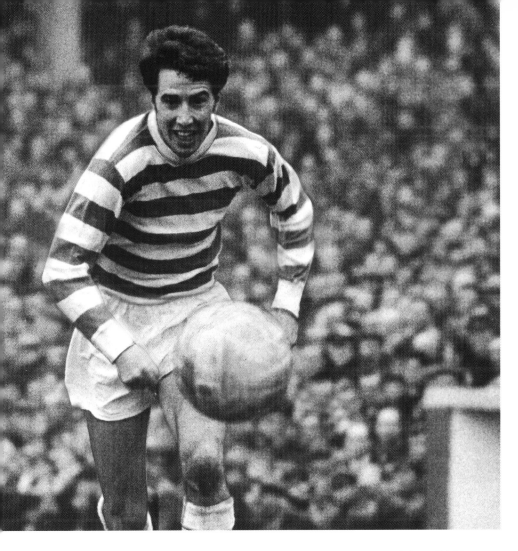

Dalglish

KENNY DALGLISH REMAINS ONE of the greatest players of his or any other era, and yet two of the greatest managers in the game either overlooked him or had their doubts – Bill Shankly of Liverpool had a young Kenny down on trial but didn't think much of the player he observed playing against Southport Reserves and sent him back home to Glasgow, whilst Jock Stein had to be convinced by his coaching staff that the player they had signed was worth persevering with.

Born in Dalmarnock in the East End of Glasgow on 4 March 1951, Kenny was raised near the docklands of Govan and grew up to be a Rangers fan! He had trials with West Ham as well as Liverpool but failed to impress, although his goal was to sign for Rangers. When a Glasgow club did show interest in him, it turned out to be Celtic, and according to legend when Jock Stein's assistant Sean Fallon turned up at the family home to persuade Kenny to join, Kenny had to tear down the Rangers posters around the house before he would let him in! It was also claimed that the signing process took rather longer than anticipated, some three hours, which did not amuse Mrs Fallon or her children who were waiting in the car outside!

He was sent out to Cumbernauld United and worked as an apprentice joiner, making the occasional first team appearance after his debut in 1968

training ground after everyone else had gone home enabling him to hone his skills. By 1972 he was a regular, being the club's top goalscorer in 1972-73 as Celtic won the League title for the eighth time in succession. The League was retained the following year and the double achieved with a Scottish Cup victory over Dundee United. A year later came success in both the Scottish Cup and League Cup, and by the time Kenny's Celtic career came to an end he had collected four League titles, four Scottish Cups and one League Cup as well as 48 caps for Scotland.

However, Kenny had joined the club just after their 1967 European Cup success and was on the club's books when they reached the Final of the 1970 competition, but the side he played for and captained seemed unlikely to enjoy major European success again.

Although Bill Shankly had been unimpressed with Kenny the first time he saw him, both he and Liverpool had sat up and taken notice when Kenny broke into the Celtic first team. According to some reports, Bill Shankly had demanded to know of his Scottish

LEFT A triumphant Kenny Dalglish at the Scottish Cup Final, 1976/77

against Hamilton. It was to take three or four years before he became a first team regular, the extra work he put in on the

ABOVE Kenny Dalglish poses for photographers with his family after receiving his MBE at Buckingham Palace

scout why Dalglish had not been recommended to Liverpool before he made his Celtic breakthrough. Shankly refused to believe that he had been responsible for passing on the player who had been on trial, convinced it must have been someone else with the same surname! When Liverpool paid a

then £400,000 to sign Kenny in the summer of 1977, Shankly had been replaced by Bob Paisley and Liverpool had just enjoyed their first European Cup success. Liverpool were able to do what Celtic couldn't in terms of European success and Kenny was to pick up three winners' medals in

Europe's premier competition as well as six English League titles, four League cups and the FA Cup once. That FA Cup victory came in 1986, when Liverpool completed the domestic double and by then Kenny had become player-manager, replacing Joe Fagan after the Heysel Stadium disaster.

There was further League and cup success to enjoy, but the events of Hillsborough in 1989, coupled with the growing pressure of being a manager, led Kenny to suddenly resign in February 1991. He would return eight months later with Blackburn Rovers, eventually taking them to the League title, and he also took Newcastle United to the FA Cup Final. Kenny did eventually return to Celtic Park, being appointed director of football in 1999, with former Liverpool club-mate John Barnes becoming head coach. After a disastrous Scottish Cup defeat by Caledonian Thistle, Barnes was relieved of his position and Kenny served as caretaker manager for the rest of the season until the arrival of Martin O'Neill.

As well as his haul of medals, Kenny set a number of international records, being the first Scottish player to win 100 caps – he eventually won 102, and is joint top scorer with 30 goals. He played in the World Cup Finals in 1974, 1978 and 1982 and was initially in the squad for the 1986 Finals in Mexico but was forced to withdraw owing to injury. He won the PFA Player of the Year award in 1983 and the Football Writers version in 1979 and 1983.

BELOW Kenny Dalglish during the Ronnie Moran Testimonial match

Deans

RIGHT John 'Dixie'
Deans

NICKNAMED 'DIXIE' IN HONOUR of the great Everton and English centre-forward, John Kelly Deans was born in Johnstone on 30 July 1946 and joined Celtic from Motherwell in 1971. When he first walked out onto the pitch wearing a Celtic shirt, against Partick Thistle in the League on 27 November 1971, there was some amusement, for Dixie never quite looked what was expected of a professional footballer – slightly overweight and with a devil may care attitude about him. Fortunately, Dixie scored on his debut in the 5-1 win and the fans took to him immediately, for he played as though he was one of them.

Whilst his Celtic career only lasted some five years there was still time enough to win two League titles, two Scottish Cups and the League Cup. He would also collect two caps for Scotland, proof that looks could sometimes be deceptive. Certainly, Dixie was as lethal in front of goal as anyone in the Scottish game at the time, hitting 124 goals in just 184 games for the club, a tally that included hat-tricks in both the Scottish Cup and League Cup Finals.

Just as Kenny Dalglish would be a year later, Dixie was lured south of the border, joining Luton Town in the summer of 1976, but managed only 14

Delaney

BORN IN STONEYBURN ON 3 September 1914, Jimmy Delaney is assured his place in the history books, having won winners' medals in the Scottish Cup with Celtic, the English FA Cup with Manchester United and the Irish FA Cup with Derry City. He missed out on achieving the ultimate clean sweep when Shamrock Rovers were beaten in the FA of Ireland Cup Final!

Jimmy joined Celtic from Stoneyburn Juniors in 1933 and made his debut the following year against Heart of Midlothian, quickly establishing himself as first choice right-winger. His speed, trickery on the ball and ability to deliver accurate crosses into the middle made him such a vital part of the side just before the Second World War, helping Celtic win two League titles and the Scottish Cup in 1937. That cup win was witnessed by the largest gathering of football spectators in European club history, with officially 146,433 paying for the privilege of watching Celtic overcome Aberdeen 2-1, but more than 5,000 were believed to have found a way of getting in for free!

appearances for the Kenilworth Road club, scoring six goals, before going on loan to Carlisle United where he made four appearances and scored two goals.

RIGHT Jimmy Delaney
playing for Manchester
United

A severely broken arm brought his Celtic career to a temporary halt in April 1939, and by the time he was fit enough to resume his playing career, the Second World War had broken out and normal League football had all but been abandoned. Jimmy remained with Celtic during the hostilities, on reduced wages, but when it was announced League football was to resume and Celtic would not increase his pay, Jimmy expressed a wish to leave the club. Matt Busby made him one of his first signings for Manchester United in February 1946 and would later claim Jimmy was the most important signing he ever made. Three times they finished runners-up in the League, but an FA Cup victory in 1948 was some consolation. Jimmy then left for Derry City, helping them win the Irish FA Cup in 1954 and, as mentioned earlier, later played for Shamrock Rovers on the other side of the border, helping them to the FA of Ireland Cup Final in 1956. It was somewhat ironic that they should be beaten by Cork Celtic in the Final, thus depriving Jimmy of his fourth winners' medal. He later returned to Scotland where he died in Lanarkshire on 26 September 1989.

Europe

ALTHOUGH EUROPEAN CLUB competition commenced in 1955, Celtic had to wait until 1962 before they made their debut, in the Inter Cities Fairs Cup. It was a rather inglorious debut too, defeat in Valencia being followed by a home draw and an early exit. Since then Celtic have performed considerably better, reaching three Finals (the European Cup twice and the UEFA Cup once), the semi-final of the European Cup twice and the same stage of the European Cup Winners' Cup twice. Here is Celtic's complete record in European competition.

*UEFA Cup total includes matches played in the Inter-Cities Fairs Cup

The 1984-85 European Cup Winners' Cup match against Rapid Vienna that Celtic won 3-0 has not been included in the above table as the result was expunged from the records by UEFA owing to crowd trouble and a replay ordered.

Competition	P	W	D	L	F	A
European Cup	110	57	19	34	186	114
European Cup Winners' Cup	38	21	4	13	76	37
UEFA Cup*	69	31	15	23	106	72
Total	217	109	38	70	368	223

European Cup

BY THE 1966-67 SEASON CELTIC had enjoyed four European campaigns, reaching the semi-finals of the European Cup Winners' Cup in 1963-64 and 1965-66. Naivety did for them in 1964, allowing MTK Budapest to come back with a 4-0 second leg win after Celtic had won the first leg 3-0. Two years later it was Liverpool who saw Celtic off, winning 2-0 at Anfield after Celtic had won 1-0 at Celtic Park. Celtic's disappointment was doubled by the fact the Final was scheduled for Hampden Park – the Final against Borussia Dortmund would have been a virtual home match!

The following season more than made up for it, Celtic's first in the premier club competition, the European Cup. FC Zurich and Nantes were despatched without too much trouble, 5-0 and 6-2 on aggregate respectively, putting Celtic into the quarter-final stage to face Yugoslavian champions Vojvodina Novi Sad. Whilst much of the season would be a march to glory courtesy of the attack, in Novi Sad it was the defence that was called into action, with only a slip by John Clark some twenty minutes before the end the only blemish of the night. Celtic were confident of overturning the one deficit in Glasgow but it took a rare defensive error by their opponents to give them a breakthrough, Pantelic dropping a cross

and Stevie Chalmers being on hand to prod the ball home. The game was entering its final minute and a play-off looked likely when Charlie Gallagher sent in a cross into the Vojvodina penalty area, with Billy McNeill rising above all others to powerfully head home the winner.

There was the prospect of another trip behind the Iron Curtain for the semi-final, this time against Dukla Prague of Czechoslovakia, but Celtic would be at home in the first leg and it would be vital to get a lead to take with them. Jimmy Johnstone gave them the lead after 27 minutes but Dukla levelled before half time. Two goals from Willie Wallace in the second leg gave Celtic a 3-1 lead to take to Prague, seemingly enough to ensure their presence in the Final. Jock Stein took no chances in the second-half however, employing a more defensive line-up for one of the only times in his career, with five in midfield preventing Dukla from creating anything at all and grinding out a 0-0 draw that booked Celtic's place in the Final in Lisbon.

There they would face Internazionale, twice winners of the trophy in 1964 and 1965 and who had gone on to win the

World Club Championship on both occasions. Celtic were making their first appearance in the Final in what was their first appearance in the competition. They had already gone further than any other British side, but although they

ABOVE Jock Stein

pressure, needlessly fouled Cappellini inside the penalty area it gave Inter the ideal opportunity to take the lead, a chance that Mazzola took despite the best efforts of Ronnie Simpson.

Such was the nature of Italian football at the time, Inter showed little inclination to further extend themselves, getting virtually every man behind the ball and confident that they could repel everything Celtic could throw at them. The one thing Jock Stein preached at half time, however, was patience – the goals would come if Celtic believed they would. The players took his words to heart, stepped up the efforts in the second-half and were rewarded when Tommy Gemmell fired home from the edge of the penalty area for an equaliser. Having got the momentum Celtic were in no mood to relinquish it and five minutes from time Stevie Chalmers pounced on Bobby Murdoch's low ball into the area to put Celtic ahead. As the Celtic players made their way back to the halfway line for the restart, they could see they had won by the defeated looks on the Inter players' faces, but Inter had been the architects of their own defeat, trying to shut up shop too early in the game.

were not there just to make up the numbers, many thought the Italians' experience would prove too much of an obstacle for even Celtic to overcome. When Jim Craig, although under

Not for the first time the holders went out at the first stage the following season, with Dynamo Kiev winning 2-1 at Celtic Park and drawing 1-1 in Kiev to win 3-2 on aggregate. In 1968-69 they reached the quarter-final stage when the other Milan club, AC, scored the only goal of the tie at Celtic Park on their way to winning the cup with a 4-1 victory over Ajax. Ajax could boast the talents of Johann Cruyff and were regarded as one of the brightest of all Dutch clubs, but they were to be pipped to European success by rivals Feyenoord, as Celtic were to discover.

The 1969-70 campaign began brightly enough, Celtic appreciating the need to keep a clean sheet in the away leg and winning the tie at home with a 2-0 victory over Basle. A 3-0 win over Benfica at Celtic Park seemed to indicate job done, but Benfica had nothing to lose and threw everything into attack in the second leg, finally

ABOVE The Celtic team line up before their European Cup Final match against Inter-Milan in Lisbon, 1967 They went on to win 2-1

The semi-final pitched the champions of Scotland against the champions of England, Leeds United, in what was already being billed as the 'Battle of Britain'. A deflected shot from George Connelly in the first minute was enough to give Celtic a 1-0 win at Elland Road, but although Celtic had the lead and deserved the victory, it was still only 'half time' in the tie. Such was the demand in Glasgow to see the conclusion of the battle, Celtic switched the game to the larger Hampden Park, with 136,505 cramming into the national stadium, the largest crowd to have witnessed any European tie. Leeds stunned the hugely partisan crowd by scoring after fourteen minutes to level the tie on aggregate, but just after half time John Hughes levelled on the night and restored Celtic's aggregate advantage with a diving header. Five minutes later Bobby Murdoch extended

drawing level on aggregate in injury time. Extra time failed to separate the two sides and it took the lottery of the toss of a coin to decide who would progress – Billy McNeill called correctly and it was Celtic into the quarter-final. Their reward was a meeting with Italian champions Fiorentina, who were beaten 3-0 at Celtic Park. This time there was to be no repeat of the Benfica debacle, Fiorentina only managing one goal in the second leg.

the score with a low, hard shot – Celtic were back into the European Cup Final.

If Celtic had been the underdogs in 1967, then Feyenoord were cast in that role in 1970. Jock Stein changed his formation for the game, switching to 4-2-4 and placing even greater emphasis on attack. Celtic took the lead through Tommy Gemmell, once again proving the worth of defenders being able to get upfield quickly enough to support the forwards, but the lead lasted only two minutes before Feyenoord equalised. The game went into extra time, with John Hughes having a perfect opportunity of winning it for Celtic soon after the additional half hour had kicked off but shot against the goalkeeper when it seemed easier to score. Three minutes from full time came Feyenoord's winner, the Dutch side using their midfield superiority to get Ove Kindvall

behind the Celtic defence to score and take the trophy.

That represented the second and so far final time Celtic reached the European Cup Final. Semi-finalists in 1973-74 and quarter-finalists in 1979-80 are as good as it has got since then, and although Celtic reached the UEFA Cup Final in 2003, it can never compare to Europe's premier competition, with every Celtic side since 1967 having to live in the shadow of the Lisbon Lions.

BELOW A forlorn Celtic supporter after his team lost the UEFA Final Cup against FC Porto, May 2003

Evans

BELOW Evans (left)
competes for the ball
during a derby match
against Rangers

BELOW Evans (left) competes for the ball during a derby match against Rangers

BORN IN GLASGOW ON 16 JULY 1927, Bobby Evans joined Celtic from St Anthony's Juniors in 1944 and made his debut in a regional League match against Albion Rovers in August of that year. Initially playing at inside-right, Bobby held his place when normal League football resumed in 1946.

The 1947-48 season was the worst in Celtic's history, with the club just one defeat away from relegation into the Second Division. In the vital last match at Dundee, Bobby was switched to half-back where it was felt his tackling abilities would better help the side – they won 3-2 to ensure safety. Manager Jimmy McGrory felt the switch would benefit Celtic in the long term and moved to make it permanent, although Bobby preferred playing in a forward position. Eventually the manager won Bobby over, pointing out that the player could provide the link between defence and attack and move further upfield as the opportunities arose. Whilst Bobby managed only ten goals during his Celtic career, his arrival in support of attack was often vital.

Over the next decade Celtic's fortunes improved, with Bobby's passing abilities the starting point for many an attack and he would go on to help the club win the League title in 1953-54, two Scottish Cups and the League Cup twice, captaining the side to victory in the 1956 League Cup against Partick Thistle. He also won 45 caps for Scotland during his time at Celtic Park and represented the Scottish League on 25 occasions. He was transferred to Chelsea in May 1960 and made 32 appearances for the 'Pensioners' and a further three for Scotland before moving on to Newport County where finished his playing career. He died in 2001.

Formation

IN EARLY 1887 THERE WAS ONLY one major Catholic club in Scotland, Hibernian, who had been formed by priests in Edinburgh in 1875 and who had adopted their name from the Roman name for Ireland. Hibernian enjoyed some success, including winning the Scottish Cup in 1887 with victory over Dumbarton. Following the victory Hibernian organised a celebration dinner, to which were invited assorted Catholic dignitaries and priests from all over Scotland.

One such priest invited was Brother Walfrid, of the Marist Order of Glasgow, who had formed a charity, The Poor Children's Dinner Table, with the idea of providing meals for the children of the East End of Glasgow, almost all of whom were poor Irish immigrants. At the Hibernian celebration, club secretary John McFadden implored those from Glasgow to form an equivalent club in the city, an idea that appealed to Brother Walfrid since it would enable the club to provide funds for his charity.

Brother Walfrid put his idea to two well-known parishioners, John McLaughlin and John Glass, and came up with the name of the football club, Celtic, the generic name that could be applied to the historical inhabitants of Scotland and Ireland. With the aid of large numbers of East

ABOVE Statue of Brother Walfrid outside Celtic FC's football ground

FORMATION

End Irish immigrants, who toiled around the clock, a stadium was built in the Parkhead district of Glasgow and just six months later was ready to stage its first match.

For their first match Celtic extended an invitation across the city to a club that was fifteen years their senior, Rangers. On 28 May 1888 Celtic's hastily assembled side of loan players, many from the Hibernian club of Edinburgh, lined up in their kit of white shirts with green collars and a red Celtic cross on the breast. The match resulted in a 5-2 win for Celtic and after the game the two sides sat down to enjoy a shared supper.

Tom and Willie Maley were given the task of strengthening the team and recruited a large number from Hibernian and one or two from the likes of Renton. Four months after their first fixture Celtic played in their first competitive match, a Scottish Cup tie against Shettleston that was won 5-1. Despite the club's relative youth, Celtic managed to make it all the way to the Final, beating a number of much older and well established clubs along the way. In the Final they came up against one of

RIGHT Patsy Gallagher

the great names of Scottish football, Third Lanark at Hampden Park.

More than 18,000 gathered at Hampden Park on 2 February 1889, including more than a fair few from the East End of Glasgow. Unfortunately a heavy snowfall made the pitch almost impossible to play on, although Third Lanark managed to keep their feet enough to register a 3-0 victory. The Scottish Football Association decided the result should not be allowed to stand and ordered a replay for the following week. This time 13,000 saw a much closer match, with Third Lanark eventually winning 2-1.

Whilst there was obvious disappointment in coming so close to winning a major trophy in their first year, Celtic's activities during that season had benefited Brother Walfrid's charity, which received the sum of £421 at the end of the season. Celtic retained their charitable status until 1895 when the committee decided to become a limited company, but the efforts of Brother Walfrid and his reasons for forming the club have never been forgotten.

Gallacher

BORN IN RAMELTON IN COUNTY Donegal on 16 March 1891, Patsy Gallacher was one of Celtic's early greats and was held to be one of the finest players of his generation, not just in Scotland but probably the world. He excelled as a schoolboy, winning some 50 trophies for various five-a-side competitions and was eventually snapped up by Clydebank Juniors.

Despite some misgivings about his abilities to succeed in professional football because of his stature – he was just 5' 6" tall and weighed some seven stone – numerous clubs made enquiries about him and he was invited to have trials with both Clyde and Celtic. His performances for Celtic, which included two goals against Dumfries and three against an Army Eleven convinced the club that he was worth signing despite his frailties and he

officially joined the club in 1911.

He made his debut against St Mirren on 2 December 1911 (according to legend, centre-forward Jimmy Quinn said to manager Willie Maley 'If you put that wee thing out on the park, you'll be done for manslaughter'), the first of 464 games for the club. He scored 192 goals during this time, including many vital goals, none more so than a header in his first Scottish Cup Final, against Clyde in April 1912 in the 2-0 win. He is best remembered, however, for his goal in his final Scottish Cup Final appearance, against Dundee in 1925, when he somersaulted over the line with the ball trapped between his feet for the equalising goal in what became a 2-1 victory. His tally of goals, especially the number of headers he scored, certainly proved that centre- and inside-forwards didn't have to be big and strapping, two

attributes that could never be levelled at Patsy Gallacher.

Known as 'The Mighty Atom', Patsy helped Celtic win the League seven times and the Scottish Cup four times, as well as collecting winners' medals in the Glasgow Cup on four occasions and the Glasgow Charity Cup eleven times when both of these competitions were an important part of the fixture list.

He won ten caps for Northern Ireland and also represented the Irish Free State against Spain in 1931 as well as being part of the Scottish Touring Party in 1927. By then he had departed Celtic, manager Willie Maley deciding in 1926 that the then 33-year-old player was past his best and allowing him to move on to Falkirk. That he gave Falkirk six years' exceptional service would indicate that Maley was perhaps a little hasty in showing Patsy the door, but it was claimed that Patsy was the highest earner at Celtic Park (even in a side that could boast the talents of Jimmy McGrory and Jimmy McStay) and Maley may well have wanted him to take a pay cut or get him off the payroll altogether. Celtic later took part in a benefit for Patsy against Falkirk in what was Patsy's final match in 1932. He died on 17 June 1952.

Gemmell

BORN IN GLASGOW ON 16 October 1943, Tommy may have played at full-back during his successful Celtic career but is chiefly remembered for his goalscoring exploits. His goals in the European Cup Finals of 1967 and 1970 helped Celtic win the trophy in 1967 and he is, along with Phil Neal of Liverpool, the only British player to have scored in two European Cup Finals.

Tommy was spotted by Celtic whilst playing for Coltness United and joined the club in 1961, making his League debut against Aberdeen in January 1963. During his initial Celtic career he was primarily used as a defensive full-back but it was Jock Stein who spotted that Tommy had a fearsome shot and instructed the player to have extra training on this aspect of his game – it was to prove extremely beneficial to Celtic in the long run.

Tommy scored four goals in Celtic's successful European Cup campaign of 1967, his other three coming in the first round ties against FC Zurich. Having started his career seldom crossing the halfway line, Tommy was often to be

found as something of an extra attacker under Jock Stein and would go on to score 63 goals in 418 matches for the club. He also helped them win four League titles, three Scottish Cups and four League Cups as well as eighteen caps for Scotland.

Despite his contribution to the 1967 European Cup win his relationship with Jock Stein was often stormy, with Stein leaving Tommy out of the League Cup Final against St Johnstone in 1969. Although he was restored to the side by the time Celtic reached the European Cup Final against Feyenoord in 1970, the relationship never quite recovered and Jock Stein allowed him to move on to Nottingham Forest in December 1971. A little over a year later he returned to Scotland to play for Dundee where he finished his playing career and had spells managing Dundee and Albion Rovers. At the height of his career, his shot was measured at 70 miles per hour.

LEFT Tommy Gemmell (second from right) scores Celtic's goal during the European Cup Final against Feyenoord, May 1970

Greatest Ever Team

CELTIC FANS VOTED FOR THEIR greatest ever eleven in 2002 and selected the following team:

1 Ronnie Simpson

2 Danny McGrain

3 Tommy Gemmell

4 Bobby Murdoch

5 Billy McNeill

6 Bertie Auld

7 Jimmy Johnstone

8 Paul McStay

9 Kenny Dalglish

10 Henrik Larsson

11 Bobby Lennox

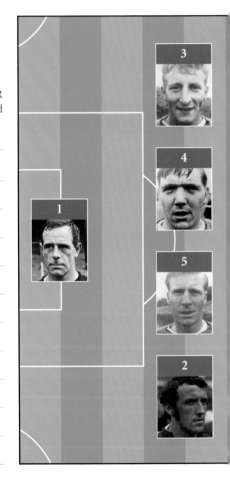

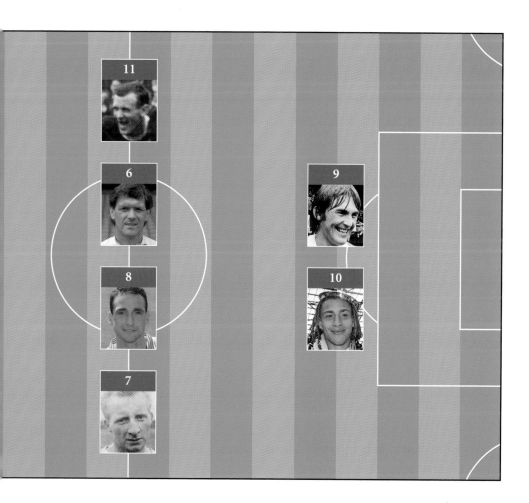

Hartson

BORN IN SWANSEA ON 5 April 1975, John began his career as a trainee with Luton Town, signing professional forms in December 1992. He was capped by Wales at Youth and Under-21 level whilst with the club and would make 54 appearances for Luton before a £2.5 million to Arsenal in January 1995. Although he made a further fifty appearances for the Gunners and broke into the Welsh first team he was unable to establish himself as a regular at Highbury, prompting a move to West Ham United in February 1997 for £3.3 million.

Off the field incidents and stiff competition for places at Upton Park saw him leave the

club in January 1999 for Wimbledon for £7 million and a further move to Coventry City in February 2001. In August of that year a £6 million move brought him to Celtic Park where he at last began to show the form that had made him one of the most expensive teenagers in the game a few years previously.

He would go on to help Celtic win three League titles, two Scottish Cups and the League Cup, linking especially well with fellow strike partners Henrik Larsson and then Chris Sutton. That he had managed to exorcise previous demons was highlighted in 2005 when he was named Player of the Year by both the PFA and FWA. He signed a new Celtic deal in January 2006 but was surprisingly allowed to leave the club for West Bromwich Albion in the summer.

LEFT Gregory Vignal challenges John Hartson during the Scottish Premiership match between Celtic and Rangers, 2004

Hay

BORN IN PAISLEY ON 29 JANUARY 1948, David Hay was hit in the eye by an arrow whilst a young boy, an incident that left him wearing contact lenses. Despite this, David omitted to tell the club when he first joined them, fearing they might show him the door if they knew about his condition!

David signed for Celtic from St Mirren Boys Guild in 1966 and made his name as one of the so called 'Quality Street Kids', the reserve team at Celtic that also boasted the likes of Kenny Dalglish, Lou Macari, Danny McGrain and George Connelly in the line-up. His League debut came against Aberdeen in March 1968 and would establish him as a regular in the side, either at full-back or pushed slightly further ahead in midfield.

A member of the side that finished runner-up in the European Cup Final in 1970, David did collect three League title medals as well as winners' medals in two Scottish Cups and one League Cup as well as 27 caps for Scotland during his time at Celtic Park. He was one of the few Scottish successes in the 1974 World Cup Finals in Germany that prompted an enquiry from Chelsea as to his availability. With Chelsea offering considerably more in basic wages than he was earning at Celtic, despite success, David opted for a move south of the border and would make 108 appearances for the Stamford Bridge club before a recurrence of his earlier eye problems forced him to retire from playing in 1979.

David then had a spell in management, taking Motherwell to promotion to the Premier League in 1981-82 before leaving in order to concentrate on running a public house in Paisley. A year later came a call to take over at Celtic Park, replacing the recently departed Billy McNeill, and David delivered the first trophy in the centenary Scottish Cup in 1985 with a 2-1 victory over Dundee United. The following season Celtic won the League for the first time since 1981-82, the finish a nail-biting 5-0 win over St Mirren whilst League leaders Hearts

were suffering broken hearts with a defeat at Dens Park against Dundee that gave Celtic the title on goal difference.

A trophy-less 1986-87 season whilst Rangers were being revitalised by Graeme Souness cost David Hay his job in the summer of 1987, making way for the returning Billy McNeill.

Honours

CELTIC HAVE WON A TOTAL OF 87 major competitions since their formation, including 40 League titles and the most prestigious of all club competitions, the European Champions Cup once. Here is a full list of their major honours.

Scottish League Champions 1893, 1894, 1896, 1898, 1905, 1906, 1907, 1908, 1909, 1910, 1914, 1915, 1916, 1917, 1919, 1922, 1926, 1936, 1938, 1954, 1966, 1967, 1968, 1969, 1970, 1971, 1972, 1973, 1974, 1977, 1979, 1981, 1982, 1986, 1988, 1998, 2001, 2002, 2004, 2006	
Scottish FA Cup winners 1892, 1899, 1900, 1904, 1907, 1908, 1911, 1912, 1914, 1923, 1925, 1927, 1931, 1933, 1937, 1951, 1954, 1965, 1967, 1969, 1971, 1972, 1974, 1975, 1977, 1980, 1985, 1988, 1989, 1995, 2001, 2004, 2005	
Scottish League Cup winners 1957, 1958, 1966, 1967, 1968, 1969, 1970, 1975, 1983, 1998, 2000, 2001, 2006	
European Champions Cup winners	1967
European Champions Cup runners-up	1970
UEFA Cup runners-up	2003
Glasgow Cup 1891, 1892, 1895, 1896, 1905, 1906, 1907, 1908, 1910, 1916, 1917, 1920, 1921, 1927, 1928, 1929, 1931, 1939, 1941, 1949, 1956, 1962, 1964, 1965, 1967, 1968, 1970, 1975*, 1982 *Trophy shared	
Glasgow Merchants and Charity Cup 1892, 1894, 1895, 1896, 1899, 1903, 1905, 1908, 1912, 1913, 1914, 1915, 1916, 1917, 1918, 1920, 1921, 1924, 1926, 1936, 1937, 1938, 1943, 1950, 1953, 1959, 1960, 1961* *Trophy shared	

RIGHT John Hughes, 1965

Hughes

BORN IN COATBRIDGE ON 3 April 1943, John Hughes joined Celtic from Shotts Bon Accord in 1959 and made his debut in the League Cup tie in August 1960 against Third Lanark, scoring Celtic's first goal in the 2-0 win. Although Celtic failed to progress out of the group stage in that competition, they did reach the Final of the Scottish Cup that season, with John scoring five of the goals that took them to Hampden Park. John was unable to score in either match against Dunfermline Athletic, the East End Park club winning 2-0 in a replay. It was not to be the last disappointment of John's career.

Initially played at centre-forward, the arrival of Jock Stein as manager in 1965 saw John switched to outside-left and receiving considerably more coaching on the abilities needed in this position than anything he had received previously. John soon developed into a speedy winger with good close ball control, able to cut inside to create even

BELOW
John Hughes,
subject of a
determined tackle

more havoc among opposition defences. When the occasion arose John could also be played at centre-forward to further confuse opponents, a ploy that worked particularly well in the European Cup clashes with Leeds United in 1970.

John, who was known as 'Yogi' within Celtic Park, as he was said to be 'smarter than the average bear' (Rangers are known as the Teddy Bears), helped

Celtic win five League titles and the Scottish Cup and League Cup once during his time with the club. He helped them reach the European Cup Finals of 1967 and 1970, although he did not play in the former and should have scored a potential winner in the latter. He did receive a winners' medal for the 1967 competition however, having played in sufficient matches along the way for his contribution to be recognised.

After the 1970 Final he asked for a change in the wage structure at the club, which relied on a low basic wage topped up with big bonuses for winning various competitions. Jock Stein's retort was that John's miss against Feyenoord (he shot directly at the keeper when it appeared easier to score) had cost Celtic the trophy and so there would be no wage increase. John sensed this also implied his time at Celtic Park was virtually at an end and in October 1971 he left for Crystal Palace having made 383 appearances for Celtic, scoring 188 goals. He had a brief spell at Selhurst Park before an even shorter stay at Sunderland, making just one appearance for the Roker Park club.

Internationals

Pat Bonner – 80 (Republic of Ireland)

Paul McStay – 76 (Scotland)

Tommy Boyd – 66 (Scotland)

Danny McGrain – 62 (Scotland)

Roy Aitken – 50 (Scotland)

Kenny Dalglish – 47 (Scotland)

Bobby Evans – 45 (Scotland)

Henrik Larsson – 43 (Sweden)

John Collins – 32 (Scotland)

Johan Mjallby – 32 (Sweden)

LEFT Pat Bonner in his Republic of Ireland strip

RIGHT Henrik Larsson playing for Sweden, celebrates after scoring in the match Sweden v England, June 2006

BELOW Paul Mcstay of Scotland on the ball

Johnston

BORN IN GLASGOW ON 30 APRIL 1963, Maurice 'Mo' Johnston is one of only a handful of players to have played for both Celtic and Rangers, although it is doubtful whether any of his contemporaries managed to attract as much controversy as accompanied Mo, for whilst they all played for Rangers and then Celtic, Mo did it the other way round – Rangers knowingly signed a Catholic for the first time.

His career had begun with quite less fanfare with Partick Thistle in 1981, netting 41 goals during his two and a half seasons with the club and prompting a move to Watford in November 1983. He appeared in the FA Cup Final the following May, which Watford lost 2-0 to Everton.

He returned north of the border later in 1984 to sign for Celtic, the club he had supported as a youngster and

helped them win the Scottish Cup at the end of the season, netting two of the goals in the semi-final against Motherwell that took Celtic to the Final. The following season saw the League title return to Celtic Park, with Mo second top goalscorer behind Brian McClair as the pair plundered 37 League goals between them. The

following season they grabbed 58 goals but Celtic slipped down to second place and finished the season empty handed.

In 1987, after 127 first team appearances and 71 goals, Mo headed across the channel to sign for Nantes on a two-year deal, initially announcing that he had no intention of ever returning to Scotland to play. At some point he had a change of mind, calling a press conference and confirming that he would be re-signing for Celtic once his contract ran out.

In July 1989 he duly returned to

Glasgow, but the press conference called to unveil him was called by Rangers, not Celtic! Those inside Celtic Park denounced him as a traitor whilst his signing for Rangers was hardly greeted with unanimous popularity inside Ibrox, with fans demonstrating outside the ground, burning scarves and tearing up season tickets as Rangers knowingly signed a Catholic player for the first time in their history. Mo Johnston acknowledged the situation he now found himself in, claiming to have done something that no Scotsman had ever done before in uniting Glasgow – both Celtic and Rangers fans now hated him! UEFA were not amused either, fining him £3,500 for 'unsporting conduct' in reneging on a deal to return to Celtic Park.

Mo made 110 appearances for Rangers before joining Everton in November 1991 for £1.5 million but spent less than a year at Goodison before returning to Scotland, with significantly less controversy, to finish his League career with Hearts and Falkirk. He finished his playing career in America with Kansas City Wizards and later became coach and

then manager to the MetroStars, a team that later became re-branded as Red Bull New York.

BELOW Mo Johnston, head coach of the New York Red Bulls

Johnstone

THERE ARE VERY FEW PLAYERS whose abilities have caused them to be mourned on both sides of the Old Firm debate upon their passing. Such is the nature of rivalry between Rangers and Celtic, but Celtic fans acknowledged the debt owed by Scottish football to Jim Baxter when he died in April 2001 just as Rangers fans joined the rest of the football world when Jimmy Johnstone lost his battle with motor neurone disease in March 2006.

Born in Viewpark in the village of Uddingston in South Lanarkshire on 30 September 1944, Jimmy was something of a childhood prodigy despite his small size and was spotted by both Celtic and Manchester United at the age of 13. Jimmy had been a ball boy at Celtic Park during the 1950s and was therefore only ever going to sign for the Celtic Park club, despite the interest from Manchester United, joining Celtic in 1961.

Despite his lack of height, standing just 5' 4" tall, Jimmy came up with a novel way of compensating by working on his stamina, undertaking 100-yard sprints in his father's pit boots. His abilities on the ball, however, were the work of football boots, able to switch the ball from one foot to the next in an instant, bamboozling defenders at the same time.

Introduced into the Celtic side in March 1963 he was a regular thereafter, going on to help Celtic win nine League titles, four Scottish Cups, five League Cups and the European Cup. Whilst domestic defenders never learned how to combat his speed and trickery, defenders on the continent were equally bemused. He was dubbed the 'Flying Flea' by one journalist, a name that stuck on the continent, whilst at home he was known as 'Jinky', supposedly in recognition of his wing style but which could be just as easily applied to his constant involvement in high jinx at both club and country level.

Although it was undoubtedly a team effort that got Celtic to the 1967 European Cup Final, Jimmy Johnstone played a huge role in their run. He later recalled what it was like lining up alongside the Internazionale side. 'There they were, Facchetti, Domenghini, Mazzola, Cappellini; all six-footers wi' Ambre Solaire suntans, Colgate smiles and sleek-backed hair. Each and every wan

o' them looked like yon film star Cesar Romero. They even smelt beautiful. And there's us lot - midgets. Ah've got nae teeth, Bobby Lennox hasnae any, and old Ronnie Simpson's got the full monty, nae teeth top an' bottom. The Italians are staring doon at us an' we're grinnin' back up at 'em wi' our great gumsy grins. We must have looked like something out o' the circus.'

Celtic of course had the last laugh and won with a style Jimmy described as 'like the Dutch speeded-up.' Whilst

BELOW Celtic fans in full voice

his reputation across the whole of Europe grew as a result of his performances, he won only 23 caps for Scotland, a ridiculously low figure given his talents. He was reported to have asked to be excluded on a number of occasions, complaining of the barracking he received from non-Celtic supporters whilst on international duty, but his involvement in a number of incidents off the field probably had international managers wary of selecting him – after one night's drinking he borrowed a rowing boat and drifted out so far he had to be rescued by the coastguard!

Jock Stein knew how to control him and how to channel his energy for the benefit of Celtic. Knowing he disliked flying, Stein promised Jimmy he would not have to travel to Yugoslavia for the second leg of a European match if Jimmy helped Celtic build up a sizeable lead in the first leg – Celtic won 5-1 and Jimmy Johnstone stayed at home.

Jimmy remained at Celtic Park until 1975 when Jock Stein decided it was time to rebuild the side. After a spell in America playing for San Jose Earthquakes he joined Sheffield United in November 1975 but made only eleven appearances for the club before moving on. He was to play for Dundee, Shelbourne and Elgin City before hanging up his boots.

In November 2001 he was diagnosed with motor neurone disease, for which there is no known cure. He helped raise funds for charity and raised awareness of the disease and even featured on a hit record with Jim Kerr of Simple Minds. In June 2005 he was honoured by having a Faberge egg designed in his honour, the first living person so honoured since the time of Tsars.

Jimmy lost his battle with the disease on March 13, 2006 and four days later thousands of fans, mainly Celtic but with contingents from virtually every other Scottish club, including a fair few from Rangers, gathered outside Celtic Park on St Patrick's Day to pay tribute. Two days later at the League Cup Final between Celtic and Dunfermline Athletic, there was a minute of applause and the entire Celtic team wore the number 7, Jimmy's old number, on both the front and back of their shorts in his memory. He would have liked that – he would have liked the 3-0 victory even more.

BELOW Raindrops run down a picture of 'Lisbon Lion' Jimmy Johnstone

Keane

ROY KEANE SPENT BARELY SIX months as a Celtic player but had sufficient impact to win League Championship and League Cup

winners' medals at the end of the season, no more than he had expected. More importantly, he fulfilled his ambition of playing for the club, something he had harboured since a schoolboy in Cork.

Born in Cork on 10 August 1971, he had begun his career with Cobh Ramblers before joining Nottingham Forest in 1990 and appearing in the FA Cup Final the following year. After Forest were relegated from the top flight in 1993 a bidding war broke out over his talents, with Manchester United paying £3.75 million to take him to Old Trafford. There he would win seven League titles and four FA Cups, but is perhaps better known for the one he missed out on – he was suspended for United's successful UEFA Champions League Final in 1999.

Made captain after the retirement of Eric Cantona, Roy was the voice of manager Sir Alex Ferguson whilst out on the pitch, cajoling his team-mates to greater effort. Unfortunately Roy sometimes carried on that role off the field and it is believed that a number of comments about his team-mates on United's own television station prompted Sir Alex Ferguson to move

FAR LEFT Roy Keane Signs for Celtic

LEFT Roy Keane is closed down by Michael McGowan during the Scottish Cup 3rd round match between Clyde and Celtic

him out of the club in December 2006. He joined Celtic on a free transfer and made his debut in the Scottish Cup match against Clyde that was surprisingly lost 2-1. Roy quickly adjusted to the pace of the Scottish game and was named man of the match in his first Old Firm derby, which Celtic won 1-0.

In May 2006 Manchester United met Celtic at Old Trafford in Roy's testimonial match, with Roy playing for Celtic in the first half and United in the second, with Manchester United winning 1-0. At the end of the season Roy accepted medical advice and retired from playing owing to a recurring hip injury.

Lambert

BORN IN GLASGOW ON 7 August 1969, Paul began his career with Linwood Rangers before joining the professional ranks with St Mirren in 1985. He was to spend eight years at Love Street before moving on to Motherwell. Although there was speculation that a number of British clubs were looking at acquiring a player who had broken into the Scottish side, it was Germany's Borussia Dortmund who bought him in 1996.

He slotted into Dortmund's midfield with ease and was one of the star performers in the club's run to the Final of the UEFA Champions League in Munich. In the Final he had the game of his life, overshadowing Juventus' playmaker Zinedine Zidane as Dortmund ran out 3-1 winners. Although he had settled in Germany and the fans had taken to him, it was no surprise when he returned to Scotland, joining Celtic in a £2 million deal in November 1997 after a little over a year playing in the Bundesliga.

He had a steadying influence on a Celtic side that had hardly started the season in good form and as the campaign progressed turned Celtic into genuine title contenders, vital if they were to prevent Rangers from winning an unprecedented ten titles in a row. With Paul providing the class in midfield and Henrik Larsson the majority of the goals, Celtic took the title by two points. That was the first of four League titles Paul won at Celtic Park, also adding two Scottish Cups and two League Cups before retiring in 2005. He had also won 40 caps for Scotland, 31 of which were awarded whilst he was with Celtic. Upon retiring he turned to coaching and management, taking over at Livingston in June 2005. He also registered as a player in case of injuries from August but resigned in February 2006 after the club had won just two matches out of 26 games.

Larsson

WIM JANSEN'S BRIEF SPELL IN charge brought the League title to Celtic Park for the first time in ten years but he will probably be better remembered for somebody he brought to the club – Henrik Larsson. At the time he was considered something of a competent rather than spectacular goal-scorer and perhaps worth no more than the £650,000 he cost the club. Over the next seven seasons he proved to be the biggest bargain the club ever landed and one of the greatest goalscorers of any age.

Born in Helsingborg in Sweden on 20 September 1971, he began his career with Hogaborgs BK in 1989 and scored 23 goals in 74 appearances, an adequate return for a player who was still learning his trade. He joined Helsingborg IF in 1992 and proved a sensation, hitting 49 goals in just 56 appearances and having a host of top European clubs making enquiries as to his availability. He was in negotiations with Grasshoppers of Zurich when Feyenoord stepped in at the last minute and paid £295,000 to take him to

Rotterdam. Whilst he struggled to score goals with the same regularity he still managed 26 in 101 appearances before falling out with the club over a contract dispute. Celtic came in with an offer of £650,000 in July 1997 to bring him to Celtic Park, one of Wim Jansen's first signings for the club.

His Celtic career hardly got off to a good start, for he was responsible for giving the ball away from which Hibernian scored one of their goals in a 2-1 win. He also scored an own goal on his European debut for the club, although Celtic managed to overcome that slip.

Gradually he settled in and started doing what he was bought to do – score at the right end, hitting one of Celtic's seven in the demolition of Berwick Rangers in the League Cup in August. He ended the 1997-98 season as top goalscorer with 19, 16 of which were netted in the League and enabled Celtic to finish as champions and thus halt Rangers' ten-in-a-row ambitions. The following season he hit 37 goals, although Celtic finished the campaign empty handed, and had hit 12 by October 1999 when he suffered a horrendous injury, breaking his leg in

two places during a UEFA Cup tie with Olympique Lyonnais. There were those who felt his career had finished and that even if he returned he would not be the same player, but after a year out of action Henrik returned to the fray and scored 53 in all competitions in the 2000-01 season, with Celtic completing the domestic treble.

The Scottish League was to return to Celtic Park in 2002 and 2004 and the Scottish Cup in 2004, although there was disappointment in 2003 when despite scoring twice in the Final Celtic lost the UEFA Cup Final against Porto 3-2. Henrik was to score 242 goals in 315 matches, a remarkable return, and one can but wonder how many he might have scored but for that year's enforced layoff.

In the summer of 2004 he left the club to join Barcelona and would help them win the Spanish League title in 2005 and 2006 and the UEFA Champions League in 2006. He returned to Celtic Park as a Barcelona player and scored against the home side but refused to celebrate his strike in recognition of the support he had received whilst with the club. His role in the UEFA Champions League Final in 2006 more than made up for it – he made one of the goals and was named man of the match, and in beating Arsenal in the Final ensured Celtic would not have to go through the qualifying rounds for the 2006-07 season's Champions League!

As well as countless goals, Henrik has collected an array of awards along the way. He won the Golden Boot award for being top European goalscorer in 2001, received an honorary degree from the University of Strathclyde in 2005 in recognition of his contribution to football and charity and was given an honorary MBE in May 2006. He was named Player of the Year by the Professional Footballers Association and the Football Writers Association in 1999 and 2001, the only player to have won both awards on two occasions, and was named Swedish Player of the Year in 1998 and 2004. He won 95 caps for Sweden, playing in the World Cup Finals on 1994, 2002 and 2006 and scoring in all three as well as the European Championships of 2000 and 2004. He even came out of international retirement to appear in the tournaments of 2004 and 2006 before finally announcing his international

retirement after Sweden's World Cup campaign of 2006. He left Barcelona at the end of the 2005-06 season to return to Sweden to finish his career.

League Positions

SEASON ENDING	POSITION	P	W	D	L	F	A	P
1891	3rd	18	11	3	4	48	21	21*
1892	2nd	22	16	3	3	62	21	35
1893	1st	18	14	1	3	54	25	29
1894	1st	18	14	1	3	53	32	29
1895	2nd	18	11	4	3	50	29	26
1896	1st	18	15	0	3	64	25	30
1897	4th	18	10	4	4	42	18	24
1898	1st	18	15	3	0	56	13	33
1899	3rd	18	11	2	5	51	33	24
1900	2nd	18	9	7	2	46	27	25
1901	2nd	20	13	3	4	49	28	29
1902	2nd	18	11	4	3	38	28	26
1903	5th	22	8	10	4	36	30	26
1904	3rd	26	18	2	6	69	28	38
1905	1st	26	18	5	3	68	31	41**
1906	1st	30	24	1	5	76	22	49
1907	1st	34	23	9	2	80	30	55
1908	1st	34	24	7	3	86	27	55
1909	1st	34	23	5	6	71	24	51
1910	1st	34	24	6	4	63	22	54
1911	5th	34	14	11	8	48	18	41
1912	2nd	34	17	11	6	58	33	45
1913	2nd	34	22	5	7	53	28	49
1914	1st	38	30	5	3	81	14	65
1915	1st	38	30	5	3	91	25	65
1916	1st	38	32	3	3	116	23	67
1917	1st	38	27	10	1	79	17	64
1918	2nd	34	24	7	3	66	26	55
1919	1st	34	26	6	2	71	22	58
1920	2nd	42	29	10	3	89	31	68
1921	2nd	42	30	6	6	86	35	66
1922	1st	42	27	13	2	83	20	67
1923	3rd	38	19	8	11	52	39	46
1924	3rd	38	17	12	9	56	33	46
1925	4th	38	18	8	12	77	44	44

SEASON ENDING	POSITION	P	W	D	L	F	A	P
1926	1st	38	25	8	5	97	35	58
1927	3rd	38	21	7	10	101	55	49
1928	2nd	38	23	9	6	93	39	55
1929	2nd	38	22	7	9	67	44	51
1930	4th	38	22	5	11	88	46	49
1931	2nd	38	24	10	4	101	34	58
1932	3rd	38	20	8	10	94	50	48
1933	4th	38	20	8	10	75	44	48
1934	3rd	38	18	11	9	78	53	47
1935	2nd	38	24	4	10	92	45	52
1936	1st	38	32	2	4	115	33	66
1937	3rd	38	22	8	8	89	58	52
1938	1st	38	27	7	4	114	42	61
1939	2nd	38	20	8	10	99	53	48
1947	7th	30	13	6	11	53	55	32
1948	12th	30	10	5	15	41	56	25
1949	6th	30	12	7	11	48	40	31
1950	5th	30	14	7	9	51	50	35
1951	7th	30	12	5	13	48	46	29
1952	9th	30	10	8	12	52	55	28
1953	8th	30	11	7	12	51	54	29
1954	1st	30	20	3	8	72	29	43
1955	2nd	30	19	8	3	76	37	46
1956	5th	34	16	9	9	55	39	41
1957	5th	34	15	8	11	58	43	38
1958	3rd	34	19	8	7	84	47	46
1959	6th	34	14	8	12	70	53	36
1960	9th	34	12	9	13	73	59	33
1961	4th	34	15	9	10	64	46	39
1962	3rd	34	19	8	7	81	37	46
1963	4th	34	19	6	9	76	44	44
1964	3rd	34	19	9	7	89	24	47
1965	8th	34	16	5	13	76	57	37
1966	1st	34	27	3	4	106	30	57
1967	1st	34	26	6	2	111	28	58
1968	1st	34	30	3	1	106	26	63
1969	1st	34	23	8	3	89	24	54
1970	1st	34	27	3	4	96	33	57

LEAGUE POSITIONS

SEASON ENDING	POSITION	P	W	D	L	F	A	P
1971	1st	34	25	6	3	89	23	56
1972	1st	34	28	4	2	96	28	60
1973	1st	34	26	5	3	93	28	57
1974	1st	34	23	7	4	82	27	53
1975	3rd	34	20	5	9	81	41	45
1976	2nd	36	21	6	9	71	42	48
1977	1st	36	23	9	4	79	39	55
1978	5th	36	15	6	15	63	54	36
1979	1st	36	21	6	9	61	37	48
1980	2nd	36	18	11	7	61	38	47
1981	1st	36	26	4	6	84	33	56
1982	1st	36	24	7	5	79	33	55
1983	3rd	36	25	5	6	90	36	55
1984	2nd	36	21	8	7	80	41	50
1985	2nd	36	22	8	6	77	28	52
1986	1st	36	20	10	6	67	38	50
1987	2nd	44	27	9	8	90	41	63
1988	1st	44	31	10	3	79	23	72
1989	3rd	36	21	4	11	66	44	46
1990	5th	36	10	14	12	37	37	34
1991	3rd	36	17	7	12	52	38	41
1992	3rd	44	26	10	8	88	42	62
1993	3rd	44	24	12	8	68	41	60
1994	4th	44	15	20	9	51	38	50
1995	4th	36	11	18	7	39	33	51
1996	2nd	36	24	11	1	74	25	83
1997	2nd	36	23	6	7	78	32	75
1998	1st	36	22	8	6	64	24	74
1999	2nd	36	21	8	7	84	35	71
2000	2nd	36	21	6	9	90	38	69
2001	1st	38	31	4	3	90	29	97
2002	1st	38	33	4	1	94	18	103
2003	2nd	38	31	4	3	98	27	97
2004	1st	38	31	5	2	105	25	98
2005	2nd	38	30	2	6	85	35	92
2006	1st	38	28	7	3	93	37	91

*Four points deducted for infringement. **Title won after a play-off with Rangers.

Lennon

BORN IN LURGAN, COUNTY Armagh on 25 June 1971, Neil Lennon began his career as a trainee with Manchester City but made just one first team appearance before joining Crewe Alexander in August 1990. Crewe manager Dario Gradi's reputation for rescuing seemingly lost careers worked its magic once again, with Neil earning rave reviews for his performances in midfield, and selection for Northern Ireland at Under-21, Under-23, B and full level during his time at Gresty Road.

After 147 appearances for Crewe he was bought by Leicester City in February 1996, where his club manager was Martin O'Neill. O'Neill assembled a hardworking and combative midfield, with Neil alongside the likes of Robbie Savage in a midfield that didn't win many friends but lots of matches, culminating in victory in the League Cup in 1997 and 2000.

Both Martin O'Neill and Neil Lennon decamped to Celtic Park in 2000, Neil joining the club he had supported as a boy. Since then he has won four League titles, three Scottish Cups and the League Cup twice, going on to become club captain. He also added to his tally of international caps, earning 40 for Northern Ireland, although he announced his retirement from international football in 2002 after receiving a death threat from a sectarian organisation. The target of considerable provocation both on and off the field, Neil has not let the matter bother him, as his performances and growing collection of winners' medals would confirm.

He was linked with a return to Leicester City in 2006 as player-manager following the dismissal of Craig Levein but chose instead to remain at Celtic and captain the side to the League title, a mission accomplished with games to spare.

Lennox

RIGHT Bobby Lennox celebrates scoring Scotland's second goal against England at Wembley, 1967

BORN IN SALTCOATS IN 1943, Bobby Lennox was playing for Ardeer Recreation when first spotted by Celtic and joined the club in 1961, going on to make his debut the following March against Dundee in the League.

Whilst Celtic at the turn of the 1960s were an ordinary side, Bobby was something of an exception, showing a devastating turn of pace that earned the nicknames 'Buzz Bomb' because of the way he went past defenders without warning or 'Lemon' because he made them look like suckers!

It was the eventual arrival of Jock Stein that turned the club's fortunes around and Bobby was an integral part of the side that would ultimately lift the European Cup in 1967. By then his reputation was known throughout the football world, with Arsenal and Leeds making enquiries to Celtic as to Bobby's availability, but Bobby only ever wanted to live in Saltcoat and play for Celtic. He did leave the club in 1978 and went to the United States to play for Houston Hurricane, netting 15 goals in 36 games, before returning to Celtic in 1979, arriving in time to help the club win the title that year and the Scottish Cup the following year.

Whilst his time with Celtic often saw new strikers arrive, all of whom were usually heralded as the latest replacement for Bobby Lennox, he invariably saw them off or formed something of a partnership with them up front. John Hughes, Stevie Chalmers, Joe McBride, Kenny Dalglish, the list is almost endless, and although Bobby was often the second striker, he weighed in with more than his fair share. Indeed, in 1967-68 he finished the season as top goalscorer, hitting 41 in all competitions, including 32 in the League, as Celtic won the title and League Cup.

By the time Bobby hung up his boots he had helped Celtic win nine League titles, six Scottish Cups and four League Cups in addition to appearing in the European Cup Final in 1967 (which was won) and 1970 (which was lost). He also appeared for Scotland ten times, including the infamous 3-2 win over England in 1967. His 589 first team appearances had brought him 273 goals, a more than adequate return. He was awarded an MBE in 1981 for his services to football and continues to serve Celtic, working as a match day host.

Maley

BROTHER WALFRID MAY HAVE been responsible for forming the club, but it was to fall to Willie Maley to give Celtic their heritage. Born William Patrick Maley in Newry, Northern Ireland on 25 April 1868, he was actually born in Newry Barracks, his father being a serving soldier in the British Army. The family were eventually posted to Scotland whilst Willie was still young and he grew up attending school in Glasgow.

He was initially more interested in athletics than in football, although he eventually showed sufficient prowess at football to be invited to play a few games for Cathcart Hazelbank Juniors in 1886, where he was spotted by Third Lanark and played a few games for them later the same year.

In 1888 he was invited to join Celtic, the new club being formed in the East End of Glasgow, and took part in their first match, a 5-2 win over Rangers. Willie and his brother Tom were entrusted thereafter with recruiting and strengthening the side, a task that would take them the length and breadth of the country looking for only the finest players to represent Celtic. Willie was no mean player himself, being in the line-up for the first League match in 1890 and their first Scottish Cup Final victory. He had also become a natural-ised Scot and would go on to win two caps for his adopted country, appearing against England and Ireland in 1893.

By 1897 Willie was no longer a first team regular but still involved with the club, helping out the committee in a number of capacities. It was at this time that the club's desire to move away from being a charitable organisation and become a limited company was at its

MALEY

highest, a move that was confirmed in March 1897. The following month, on 3 April 1897, Willie Maley was appointed secretary-manager of Celtic, the first manager the club had.

Since the League title was won at the end of his first season in charge, the move was an obvious success, but in truth managers in the Victorian era were completely different from their modern day counterparts – Willie Maley did not organise tactics or take the players training. He did not work out moves or formations to outwit the opposition. He didn't even tell the players face to face whether they were in or out of the side for the next match – they learned whether they had been selected from the line-up printed in the newspaper! Willie Maley did make a number of changes at the club, however. The Celtic he had joined and played for for a little over ten years had been a buying club, paying good money to acquire some of the brightest talents from around the country. Under Maley, Celtic came to rely on developing their own talents, scouring junior football for youngsters he could bring in relatively cheaply and mould into Celtic players.

The first great side Willie Maley fashioned featured such illustrious names as Jimmy McMenemy, Alex McNair and Jimmy Quinn and won the League titles six seasons in succession between 1905 and 1910 and collected the first domestic double of Scottish League and Cup. Six titles in a row remained a record until beaten by Celtic in the 1970s. When this team grew old Willie Maley fashioned a new one, bringing in the likes of Patsy Gallacher and won a further four consecutive titles between 1914 and 1917, during which they set a record run of 62 games without defeat, of which 49 were won and 13 drawn between November 1915 and April 1917.

The Patsy Gallacher-led side won two further titles in 1919 and 1922 before Willie Maley began assembling his third great side, one that would feature Jimmy Delaney and Jimmy McGrory and win the League in 1936 and 1938 and the Scottish Cup in 1937. After the 1938 League title win, in what appropriately enough was Celtic's Golden Jubilee, Willie Maley addressed the audience at the dinner held in the club's honour and described his own fifty years at the club as a labour of love. His service was marked by the club with a gift of 2,500 guineas, 50 for each of his years with the club.

Whilst the Jubilee dinner had been a happy occasion, the fall out between Celtic and Willie Maley began almost as soon as the money was handed over. It was, as Maley pointed out, the first such benefit he had ever received from the club and he believed Celtic should pay the tax due. The board in turn had no intention of paying the tax and, concerned that Rangers were becoming a more healthier rival, also wanted to make a change at the helm of the club, reasoning that as he was approaching 70, a younger man would help maintain the club's position. The board eventually won out, severing their ties with the then 71-year-old Willie Maley in December 1939. Whilst his great rival across the city at Rangers, Bill Struth, would eventually join the board at Ibrox, no such position was to be found for Willie Maley – once he was out, he was out for good.

He had been manager of the club for 43 years and had delivered no fewer than 16 League titles, 14 Scottish Cups, 14 Glasgow Cups and 19 Glasgow Charity Cups. He had, almost single-handedly, turned Celtic into one of the most successful and famous clubs in the game and given the club a heritage it could be more than proud of.

BELOW Willie Maley, stalwart manager in the nineteenth and twentieth centuries

Managers

ONLY FIVE DIFFERENT MEN managed Celtic in the first one hundred years after their formation, which was later followed by six in nine years! Here is the complete list of those who have managed Celtic.

Manager	Year
Willie Maley	1897 to 1940
Jimmy McStay	1940 to 1945
Jimmy McGrory	1945 to 1965
Jock Stein	1965 to 1978
Billy McNeill	1978 to 1983
David Hay	1983 to 1987
Billy McNeill	1987 to 1991
Liam Brady	1991 to 1992
Lou Macari	1992 to 1994
Tommy Burns	1994 to 1997
Wim Jansen	1997 to 1998
Jozef Venglos	1998 to 1999
John Barnes	1999 to 2000
Martin O'Neill	2000 to 2005
Gordon Strachan	2005 to date

McBride

BORN IN GLASGOW ON 10 JUNE 1938, Joe McBride was to be Jock Stein's first signing as Celtic manager, joining the club in a £22,500 deal in the summer of 1965 after starring against Celtic in the Scottish Cup semi-final whilst playing for Motherwell. Equally good in the air and on the ground, he had run Celtic ragged in the two meetings between the clubs before Celtic finally triumphed 3-0 in the replay.

He began his Celtic career in blistering form, netting 31 League and 12 Cup goals in the 1965-66 season as Celtic won the League and League Cup. The following season was following a similar pattern too, with Stein swooping for Willie Wallace from Hearts to further bolster the attack. It was his intention to pair McBride and Wallace up front, but a cartilage injury sustained by Joe in the match against Aberdeen on Christmas Eve 1966 would keep him out for the rest of the season. Although he had already scored 35 goals, a tally that was not beaten until the very last match of the season, Celtic's European Cup Final victory, achieved without Joe McBride, completely overshadowed his efforts that campaign. He did receive a winners' medal, however, having appeared in sufficient games in the early rounds to merit an award.

Although Joe returned to first team duty with Celtic again he was not the same player and made sporadic appearances for the club before moving on to Hibernian in 1968, having scored 86 goals in just 93 appearances and won two League titles, two League Cups and two caps for Scotland. He later played for Dunfermline and Clyde before retiring in 1972.

BELOW Joe McBride heading in the gallows

McGrory

WIDELY REGARDED AS ONE OF the greatest Celtic players of all time, Jimmy McGrory would later return to the club as manager, a position he was to hold for nearly twenty years. Born in Glasgow on 26 April 1904, Jimmy was spotted whilst playing for St Rochs Juniors and joined Celtic in 1921 and made his debut against Third Lanark in January 1923.

A loan spell with Clydebank enabled him to hone his skills, returning to Celtic Park destined to become the club's greatest ever goalscorer. It was not just the quantity that he scored, 550 in first class matches, but the quality, with many of them being spectacular efforts. Jimmy was not afraid to try for goal from anywhere, with one of his team-mates commenting that Jimmy could head the ball further than most players could kick.

He was top goalscorer in the Scottish League in 1927, 1928 and again in 1936, proof that the passage of time had done little to blunt his prowess. His tally for 1927 was a new record for the Scottish League, 47 goals, and the following

campaign was just one less. Celtic had a goalscoring sensation on their hands, which the board and manager Willie Maley decided to cash in, offering the player to Herbert Chapman of Arsenal for £10,000. Fortunately for Celtic, Jimmy declined to move south, preferring to remain at Celtic Park (to ensure the transfer would not go through, he asked Arsenal for a £2,000 signing on fee when the legal limit was £650), but the board got their revenge in a slightly underhand way. Denied a big transfer fee following the player's decision to stay put, Celtic paid him significantly less than his team-mates for the remainder of his Celtic career, almost another ten years!

Jimmy put the matter behind him and carried on doing what he did best, scoring goals. He beat his own League record in 1936, hitting 50 as Celtic won the League title for the first time in ten years. In all Jimmy was to win three League titles and four Scottish Cups as well as seven caps for Scotland, the latter a

ridiculously low figure for a striker with his talents.

His final game for Celtic came in October 1937 against Queen's Park, with Jimmy signing off with a hat-trick in the 4-3 win. That took his Celtic tally to 395 goals in 378 games in the League and 468 goals in 445 games, figures that are still a record for the club. Upon retiring from playing Jimmy took over as manager of Kilmarnock, a position he was to hold until 1945 when invited back to Celtic Park to take over as manager from Jimmy McStay.

Jimmy was manager of the club for nearly twenty years, until he in turn was replaced by Jock Stein in March 1965. Whilst his time in charge was not as successful as many had expected or would have liked, bringing just one League title (in 1954), two Scottish Cups and two League Cups, he did provide the club with a steadying hand during his time in charge. When Jock Stein returned to take over as manager in March 1965, Jimmy became the club's first public relations officer, a position he was to hold until his death on 20 October 1982.

McMenemy

BORN IN RUTHERGLEN IN 1880, Jimmy McMenemy led the Celtic forward line in the years following the turn of the century, helping them become the first truly great Celtic side. He was playing for Rutherglen Glencairn when spotted by the club and joined in 1902, making his debut that November against Port Glasgow.

Whilst his eventual tally of 144 League goals is undoubtedly impressive, Jimmy's game was such that he was more often than not a provider of chances for others, his leadership role being recognised in his nickname, 'Napoleon'. In a Celtic career that was to last eighteen years, he helped win the League title ten times and the Scottish Cup six times, including the memorable 1904 Final against Rangers where Celtic came from being 2-0 down to win 3-2.

He initially retired at the age of 37 but was back a year later to help the club win the 1919 League title and then moved on to Partick Thistle. There he added another Scottish Cup winners' medal to his collection,

helping them overcome Rangers in the 1921 Final. Jimmy was to return to Celtic Park in 1935, joining the coaching staff for five years until the Second World War broke out. His son John also won a Scottish Cup winners' medal with Celtic in 1927. He died in 1965 at the age of 85.

RIGHT A stern Jimmy McMenemy

McNamara

BORN IN GLASGOW ON 24 October 1973, Jackie McNamara began his professional career with Dunfermline Athletic before a £600,000 deal took him to Celtic Park in 1995, the club his father had played for some twenty years earlier.

Jackie's progress was such he was named Young Player of the Year by the PFA in 1996, but following the arrival of Martin O'Neill as manager Jackie had to be content with playing more of a bit part in the Celtic side. He eventually won over his manager to become a regular in the side, culminating in being named Player of the Year by the FWA in 2004.

He was named captain of the side when Paul Lambert was injured and would go on to help the club win four League titles, the Scottish Cup three times and the League Cup three times and won thirty caps for Scotland. Although Gordon Strachan identified Jackie as a vital member of the squad and a player the club needed to keep at Celtic Park, disagreements over a new contract meant he left Celtic on a Bosman free transfer in the summer of 2005 for Wolverhampton Wanderers.

ABOVE
Jackie McNamara is challenged by Thomas Buffel of Rangers during the Tennants Scottish Cup 3rd round match, 2005

McNeill

TO MANY PEOPLE BILLY MCNEILL is Celtic, having given the club exceptional service as both a player and manager over almost fifty years. He was born in Bellshill on 2 March 1940 and played for local junior side Blantyre Victoria before signing with Celtic in 1957, making his debut the following October against Clyde in the League Cup.

As a defender he was more often concerned with preventing the opposition from scoring, but Billy could also be relied upon to score some vital goals of his own, none more so than the winner in the Scottish Cup Final against Dunfermline Athletic in 1965 that delivered Jock Stein's first trophy as Celtic manager.

A natural born leader, Billy was made captain of the club and would collect more trophies than any other captain in the club's history. The most notable trophy he collected was of course the European Cup in 1967, but there were still many more presentations before he finally retired from playing in 1975 – he was to win nine League Championships, seven Scottish Cups and six League Cups during his time at Celtic Park.

Known by the players as 'Cesar', after the film star Cesar Romero (Billy didn't look much like the film star, but the players gave him the moniker after seeing the film 'Ocean's Eleven', in which Romero was the getaway driver – Billy was one of the few players at the club to own a car at the time!), Billy came to personify Celtic – in 790 appearances for the club he was sent off just once, a remarkable figure for a player who played every match as though it were a Cup Final. Following his retirement he became manager of Clyde and then Aberdeen before returning to Celtic in 1978 and guiding them to three League titles, the Scottish Cup and League Cup in his five years in charge.

Billy then took over as manager of Manchester City and later Aston Villa before returning to Celtic for a second spell in 1987 for four years. This tenure brought one League title and two Scottish Cups before he was replaced by Liam Brady. Billy later had a brief spell in charge at Hibernian and also unsuccessfully stood as a candidate for the Scottish Senior Citizens Unity Party in the 2003 election for the Scottish Parliament. He was, however, awarded an MBE in recognition for his services to football.

McStay

BORN IN HAMILTON ON 22 October 1964, Paul McStay spent his entire professional career with Celtic, giving the club sixteen years of exceptional service. An exceptional and reliable performer, Paul was one of the few positives in what were trying times for the club as they attempted to regain their former dominance of the domestic game and his career deserved considerably more honours than it achieved.

He joined Celtic from Celtic Boys Club as a seventeen-year-old and made his debut in January 1982 against Queen of the South in a Scottish Cup tie. His League debut came a week later and Paul marked the occasion by scoring Celtic's third in a 3-1 win at Pittodrie. It was the first of 57 League goals he was to score for the club and at the end of the season he had collected his first honour as Celtic retained the League title.

Further League titles were added in 1986 and 1988, with his midfield

RIGHT Paul Mcstay in action

FAR RIGHT
Paul McStay pictured in 1996

performances earning him the nickname 'The Maestro', a fitting name for a player who was the driving force behind the championship win during the club's centenary season. He also won four Scottish Cups and the League Cup once during his time with the club and holds the distinction of being the most capped Scottish player at the club, having won 76 caps for his country. Although it was widely believed Paul was on his way to Italy to play at the end of the 1991-92 season, he chose to remain with Celtic. He would go on to make 677 first team appearances before injury brought about his retirement in 1997. He was awarded the MBE for his services to football.

Murdoch

HE HAD PLENTY TO CHOOSE from but Jock Stein always claimed that Bobby Murdoch was the best player in Britain during the 1960s, the highest praise the Celtic manager could give to any player. Yet Bobby Murdoch was perhaps worthy of the accolade, for his midfield partnership with Bertie Auld made the Celtic side of his era one of the greatest club sides of any era.

Born in Bothwell on 17 August 1944, he was playing for Cambuslang Rangers when spotted by Celtic and signed with the club in 1959. His debut came three years later, against Hearts in a League Cup tie in August 1962, the first of 484 first team appearances for the Celtic Park club.

His talents complimented those of Bertie Auld to perfection, with Bobby able to control and influence a match at will, upon which came a multitude of successes both domestically and in Europe. A member of Celtic's two European Cup Final teams, Bobby's contribution to the 1967 Final was a key

component in their eventual victory. There were also to be winners' medals from seven League titles, four Scottish Cups and four League Cups as well as twelve caps for Scotland, a small figure given his importance to Celtic.

Bobby remained with the club until 1973 when he left to join Middlesbrough, making 125 appearances for the club before his retirement in 1976. He then served as coach of the junior side and had a brief spell as manager that ended with the club being relegated. He left soon after and had an unsuccessful time as a publican. He later returned to Celtic Park as a match day host but was sadly to die following a stroke on 15 May 2001, the first of the Lisbon Lions to pass away.

Nakamura

BORN IN YOKOHAMA ON 24 JUNE 1978, Shunsuke Nakamura, widely regarded as one of the most important members of the Japanese national team, joined Celtic from Reggina of Italy for £2.5 million in the summer of 2005.

He had begun his career with Yokohama Marinos in 1997 and broke into the Japanese national team in 2000, going on to help them win the Asian Cup the same year and retain it four years later. This was despite being dropped from the squad for the 2002 World Cup in Japan and South Korea, with his national manager claiming he did not have the physical presence to justify inclusion. He more than made up for that with his sublime ball skills, which were of sufficient quality to have one former manager, Steve Perryman, claiming 'he could open a tin of beans with his left foot.'

His physical abilities improved after a three year spell in the Italian Serie A, with his creative abilities subsequently prompting a move to Celtic in 2005. He has coped well with the demands of the Scottish Premier League, helping the club win the title at the end of his first season and adding the League Cup for good measure. Restored to the national side for the 2006 World Cup, he scored Japan's opening goal in their match against Australia.

RIGHT Midfielder Shunsuke Nakamura

Nicholas

'CHAMPAGNE CHARLIE' NICHOLAS first burst onto the scene as a teenager in 1980, hitting sixteen League goals for the club in his first campaign. He was born in Glasgow on 30 December 1961 and joined Celtic Boys Club before joining the professional ranks in 1979.

After his initial burst of activity he was sidelined with illness and then a broken leg but returned to the first team and the scoresheet during the 1982-83 season, going on to hit 48 goals in all competitions that term. That prompted considerable speculation that he might be on his way south of the border and Celtic eventually accepted a £625,000 offer from Arsenal in July 1983.

Although he scored both of the goals that earned Arsenal the League Cup in 1987, his work rate was always going to be something of a problem for a manager like George Graham and he eventually returned to Scotland to sign for Aberdeen in January 1988. There he rediscovered his form that ultimately led to a return to Celtic Park in 1990

LEFT Charlie Nicholas in action during a match against Everton at Celtic Park

and whilst he had lost some of his pace, he was still a goalscorer of considerable note. By the time he moved on to Clyde in 1996 he had taken his tally of Celtic goals to 125 in 209 first team appearances. He retired from playing in 1996 and subsequently became a pundit for Sky TV.

Old Firm

CELTIC AGAINST RANGERS ARE three words that sum up the most intense club rivalry in the world, a match that neither side dare lose for fear of giving up bragging rights until the next meeting between the two foes. Whilst the fixture was more than just a football clash for many years, with Celtic cast as the flag bearers for Catholics and Rangers for Protestants, the meetings between the two clubs have returned to being just about football in recent years, a welcome move.

If the clubs have existed for nearly one hundred years as the best of enemies, then it wasn't always the case. Indeed, for many years relations between the two clubs were more than cordial, with Rangers providing the opposition to Celtic in Celtic's very first match, whilst later chairman John H McLaughlin, a more than talented

pianist, would often accompany the Rangers Glee Club and did so for several years.

Celtic's side for their very first match, on 28 May 1888 was entirely made up of guests, with Neilly McCallum having played for Rangers a few months earlier in a friendly fixture against Aston Villa. He would score the first goal in what became a 5-2 win for Celtic over Rangers and after the match the two sides, together with officials, sat down and enjoyed supper and a concert at St Mary's Hall, with Celtic toasting their

better of their rivals in the first League matches between them, Celtic drawing 2-2 at home and winning 2-1 away.

Having first met in the Scottish Cup Final in 1894 (3-1 to Rangers) the relationship between the two began to turn sour in 1898. The New Year's Day battle between the top two sides in the League drew a crowd of 50,000 to Celtic Park, yet there were just 40 or so policemen on duty to try and maintain order. There were several pitch invasions, culminating in one last one on seventy minutes that saw the game being abandoned with the score at 1-1. There was considerable criticism aimed at Celtic over their inability to control their fans, but Rangers were apparently more concerned that Celtic refused to share the gate money 50/50 as had supposedly been agreed, receiving instead the standard 20%.

Following the Ibrox disaster of 1902, Rangers organised a four team competition involving them, Celtic, Sunderland and Everton in what became billed as the British League Cup. The trophy for the competition was the Exhibition Cup, a trophy that had been won by Rangers in 1901 after an eight team competition, beating Celtic in the

LEFT Chris Burke of Rangers is tackled by Mark Wilson of Celtic during a League match between Rangers and Celtic, 2006

opponents and vice versa in what was by all accounts an entertaining evening.

Although Celtic lost their next match against Rangers, another friendly stage in August 1888, they had the upper hand over their rivals in early competitive clashes, winning 6-1 in the quarter-final of the Glasgow Cup in October 1888 at Ibrox, still their biggest ever victory at Rangers' ground, and a 1-0 win in the first round of the Scottish Cup in September 1890, a match that attracted 16,000 to Celtic Park with a further 5,000 being locked out. Celtic also had the

Final. The two Glasgow rivals met in the Final of the British League Cup, with Celtic winning 3-2 after extra time, but what caused the controversy between the two sides was Celtic's refusal to put the trophy, which Rangers believed was rightfully theirs, up for annual competition. The trophy, the cause of much aggravation in 1902, remains at Celtic Park to this day.

The occasional spat aside, the rivalry between the two clubs is at its most intense at fan level. There have been numerous pitch invasions at matches involving the two, with one of the worst being immediately after the 1980 Scottish Cup Final, which Celtic won 1-0 after extra time thanks to a goal from George McCluskey. When the Celtic players went over to the end where their fans were congregated to celebrate, hoards of Rangers fans invaded the pitch and engaged in bitter battle on the pitch against their foes. Although both clubs were subsequently fined (a paltry £20,000 each), legislation was introduced in the shape of the Criminal Justice (Scotland) Act 1980 that went some considerable way to removing the stain of crowd violence from the Scottish game. Future battles on the field of play have thus been confined to eleven players wearing Rangers kit and eleven Celtic counterparts.

If every Celtic victory over Rangers is one to be savoured, then there are some that are elevated to the simply memorable. Although the numbers of those who will have witnessed at first hand Celtic's 7-1 demolition of their greatest rivals in the League Cup Final of 1957 diminishes year on year, the story of the day will live on forever. Sammy Wilson and Neil Mochan gave Celtic a two goal lead going into the interval, but Rangers were still seemingly in the game having created a number of chances themselves. McPhail headed a third soon after the restart before Rangers reduced the arrears, but Celtic were in rampant form on the day and were not to be denied further goals. Billy McPhail would eventually go on to complete his hat-trick, Mochan took his tally to two and in the final minute Billy McPhail was fouled in the area to earn Celtic a penalty. Willie Fernie, whose midfield prompting had been the architect behind the victory, fired home a low penalty to complete the scoring. For many years Celtic fans delighted in reminding Rangers fans of the time – seven past Niven.

FAR LEFT Celtic fans during the Scottish Premier League match against Rangers

BELOW A police officer walks in front of supporters at a match between Rangers and Celtic

O'Neill

THE NEXT DECADE FOLLOWING the departure of Billy McNeill after his second spell in charge at Celtic Park was not a pleasant one for Celtic fans as a succession of managers, many of them big names (at least as players) arrived

and subsequently vacated the manager's chair, each of them having promised to restore the club to former glories and failing. In the summer of 2000 came the latest, former Wycombe Wanderers, Norwich City and Leicester City manager Martin O'Neill.

Born in Kilrea in County Londonderry on 1 March 1952, Martin had had a distinguished playing career with Nottingham Forest, helping them with the League title, two League Cups and two European Cups. He was also a Northern Ireland international, having won 62 caps for his country, and finished his playing career with Norwich City and Manchester City before turning to management. After a spell in non-League circles he guided Wycombe Wanderers to promotion to the Football League before moving on to Leicester City, where he fashioned a side good enough to maintain their Premier League status and win two League Cups.

He brought to Celtic Park something of a new formation for the club, 3-5-2, which made the side defensively solid and able to get men up front quickly to support the attack, a tactic that worked to perfection in Martin's first Old Firm clash – Celtic won 6-2. At the end of his first season in charge Celtic won the treble, finishing fifteen points ahead of Rangers in the League. That lead was extended the following season to 18 as Celtic became the first side to top 100 points in a season – they finished with 103 – in retaining the title for the first time since 1982.

There was to be further silverware to savour during his five-year tenure, with seven trophies in all being won – three League titles, two Scottish Cups and two League Cups, but it was the fact that he restored some of Celtic's European tradition for which he will always be remembered, taking the club to the UEFA Cup Final in 2003 before an extra time defeat by Porto.

As he brought continued success to Celtic Park there was constant speculation that he would be on his way, with a succession of clubs in England believed to be interested in making him their manager. Martin did announce his intention to leave Celtic at the end of the 2004-05 season, but it was not to take over at another club – Martin was to look after his wife Geraldine as she battled lymphoma.

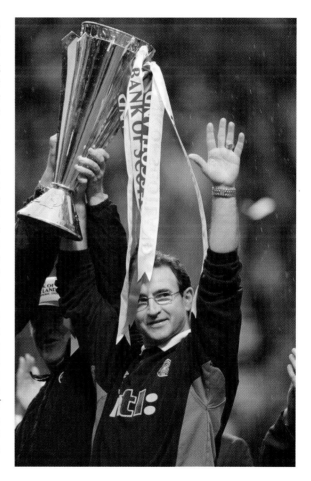

Petrov

BORN IN MONTANA, BULGARIA on 5 July 1979, Stilian Petrov was brought to Celtic in 1999 by John Barnes but struggled to make much of an impact initially, seemingly another player who got lost in the confusion that reigned at Celtic Park at the time.

It was to take the arrival of Martin O'Neill as manager in the summer of 2000 before Celtic fans started to see the best of the former CSKA Sofia midfielder, with Martin utilising the player's undoubted talents in a midfield roving role, one that enabled him to provide the link between midfield and attack and made Celtic such a potent force during Martin O'Neill's reign.

A member of the side that won the League title in 2001, 2002, 2004 and 2006 Stilian, known to his team-mates as Stan, also helped win the Scottish Cup in 2001, 2004 and 2005 and the League Cup in 2001 and 2006. There is, however, speculation that the player, a full Bulgarian international with more than 50 caps to his name, has suffered a breakdown in relations with manager Gordon Strachan and handed in a written transfer request in April 2006, despite having a contract that runs until 2009.

Player of the Year

THE SCOTTISH FOOTBALL Writers Association introduced their Player of the Year award in 1965, with Celtic's Billy McNeill the very first winner. The following Celtic players have won the award.

1965 – Billy McNeill
1967 – Ronnie Simpson
1969 – Bobby Murdoch
1973 – George Connelly
1977 – Danny McGrain
1983 – Charlie Nicholas
1987 – Brian McClair
1988 – Paul McStay
1998 – Craig Burley
1999 – Henrik Larsson
2001 – Henrik Larsson
2002 – Paul Lambert
2004 – Jackie McNamara
2005 – John Hartson

LEFT
Henrik Larsson

BELOW
A happy
Shaun Maloney

PLAYER OF THE YEAR

The players union, the PFA, instigated its own award in 1978, voted for by all professional players. The following Celtic players have won the award.

1980 – Davie Provan	
1983 – Charlie Nicholas	
1987 – Brian McClair	
1988 – Paul McStay	
1991 – Paul Elliot	
1997 – Paolo Di Canio	
1998 – Jackie McNamara	
1999 – Henrik Larsson	

2000 – Mark Viduka

2001 – Henrik Larsson

2004 – Chris Sutton

2005 – John Hartson (jointly with Fernando Ricksen of Rangers)

2006 – Shaun Maloney

ABOVE Davie Provan

ABOVE RIGHT Craig Buley

RIGHT Jackie McNamara

FAR RIGHT Paul Lambert

Quinn

BORN IN CROY ON 8 JULY 1878, Jimmy was playing for Smithson Albion when first spotted by Celtic, but Celtic manager Willie Maley had to be patient to land his man. Jimmy soon proved more than capable of making the step up to the professional game, although it took some time before he started scoring with any great regularity, mainly because Celtic used him as a winger for the first three years or so of his time at the club.

Standing just 5' 8" tall, Jimmy relied on a number of attributes to make up for his lack of inches; his speed, both with and without the ball, ability to be in the right position at the right time, his bravery and a tenacious attitude would eventually make him the ideal centre-forward. Despite his height he scored a fair number of goals with headers, a further ability he worked hard at in training.

The Jimmy Quinn reputation is largely built on the strength of one match – the 1904 Scottish Cup Final that Rangers were leading 2-0 at half time, only for Jimmy to take over in the second half and score a hat-trick (it may well have been the first hat-trick in a Scottish Cup Final, but it was certainly the first in an Old Firm Final) that prompted the belief that no match was lost until Jimmy Quinn left the field.

By the time Jimmy retired in 1915 it was with six League Championships and four Scottish Cup winners' medals to his name, as well as eleven caps for Scotland. More crucially, his 331 appearances for Celtic had resulted in 217 goals, a phenomenal return. Even in the 1930s, when Jimmy McGrory was at his peak, manager Willie Maley still claimed Jimmy Quinn 'the greatest centre-forward we have ever possessed.' A coal miner either side of his Celtic career, Jimmy died in November 1945.

BELOW Jimmy Quinn

Quotes

"I feel we have the players fit to wear the mantle of champions of Europe. I have told them so. Now they know it's up to them."

Jock Stein

"As soon as I scored that goal, the Italian players' heads went down. They didn't want to know after that. They knew the writing was on the wall."

Tommy Gemmell

"We can have no complaints. Celtic deserved their victory. We were beaten by Celtic's force. Although we lost, the match was a victory for sport."

Helenio Herrera, Inter Milan manager after the 1967 European Cup Final.

"We won and we won on merit. This win gives us more satisfaction than anything. I can still hardly believe it's true."

Jock Stein after the 1967 European Cup Final.

"John, you're immortal."

Bill Shankly to Jock Stein after the 1967 European Cup Final.

"I don't think he knew what he was going to do next, so what chance did the opposition have?"

Tommy Gemmell on Jimmy Johnstone.

"It is up to us, to everyone at Celtic Park, to build up our own legends. We don't want to live with history, to be compared with legends from the past. We must make new legends."

Jock Stein in 1966.

"When the Rangers game came round, for instance, and they were going to give you £1,000 if you won, that was a driving force to get players to play. If you were on £55 a week and had a chance to earn £1,000, you would kill, wouldn't you?"

Lou Macari on Celtic's bonus structure in the 1970s.

"I am often asked how this Rangers team compares with the Lisbon Lions. I have to be honest and say I think it would be a draw, but then, some of us are getting on for 60."

Bertie Auld on Rangers' 1993 side.

"I hit the ball against the goalkeeper. It

was just one of those things but I reckon that, when I did that, that was me finished at Celtic. Jock Stein was like that: he tended to blame you for things. Within a year I had left the club."

John Hughes on his miss against Feyenoord in the 1970 European Cup Final.

"I don't believe 50,000 fans will travel to Seville. That is madness. It is an exaggeration. I think a fair number will be around 4,000. We are talking about a Final to be played on a Wednesday, a day when people normally work."

Rafael Carmona, UEFA security chief before the 2003 UEFA Cup Final – nearly 80,000 Celtic fans turned up in Seville.

"The best place to defend is in the other team's penalty box."

Jock Stein

Records

Record victory
11-0 v Dundee, Scottish League,
26/10/1895

Record defeat
0-8 v Motherwell, Scottish League,
30/4/1937

Most League points
103 in Scottish Premier League in
2001-02 (under three points for a win),
72 in Scottish League in 1987-88
(under two points for a win)

Most League goals
116 in Scottish League in 1915-16

Highest League scorer in a season
Jimmy McGrory, 50 goals in Scottish
League 1935-36

Most League goals in total aggregate
Jimmy McGrory, 395 goals,
1923-1937

Most League appearances
Alec McNair, 548,
1905-1925

Most capped player
Pat Bonner, 80 appearances
for the Republic of Ireland

Record transfer fee received
£4.7 million from Sheffield Wednesday
for Paolo Di Canio, 1997

Record transfer fee paid
£6 million to Chelsea for Chris Sutton,
2000

LEFT Chris Sutton celebrates scoring a penalty during a League match between Celtic and Dundee Utd, 2004

Simpson

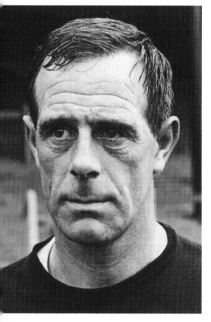

BORN IN GLASGOW ON 11 October 1930, Ronnie Simpson was seemingly in the twilight of his career when he joined Celtic in 1964, having already given sterling service in goal for the likes of Queen's Park, Third Lanark, Newcastle United and Hibernian before arriving at Celtic Park.

He had begun his career with Queen's Park just as the Second World War was coming to an end and would go on to be a member of the Great Britain side for the 1948 Olympics. His reputation was effectively made at Newcastle United, helping them win the FA Cup in 1952 and 1955 and he returned to Scotland to sign for Hibernian in 1960.

He was already 34 years of age when Hibernian manager Jock Stein sold the player to Celtic, with Ronnie seen as cover for John Fallon. When it was announced that Jock Stein was to return to Celtic Park as manager in 1965, Ronnie could have been forgiven for thinking his Celtic career was at an end. Initially Jock Stein kept Fallon in the side but eventually, needing much more experience than Fallon could provide, gave Ronnie his chance, a chance Ronnie grabbed with both hands.

Known within the club as 'Father', on account of his age, Ronnie proved a more than capable goalkeeper for the club, helping them win four League titles, one Scottish Cup and three League Cups as well as the European Cup in 1967. That same year he even made his Scotland debut, keeping goal in the 3-2 win over world champ-ions England at Wembley. He would go on to win five caps, proving that goalkeepers did get better with age.

He finally retired in 1970 having made 188 first team appearances for the club and would go on to briefly manage Hamilton Academical for a year. He died on 19 April 2004 from myocardial infarction.

Stein

JOCK STEIN WOULD BE CON-
sidered a Celtic legend if we only took his
playing career into account, but his
exploits as a manager surpassed everything and ensured he is considered one
of the greatest managers of all time.

Born in Burnbank on 5 October 1922,
Jock worked in a carpet factory and
down the mines before football gave him
an escape from a life of drudgery.
He signed with Blantyre Victoria in 1938
and began his professional career with
Albion Rovers in 1942, although he
continued working down the mines
during the week whilst playing at
the weekend.

After a spell on loan with Dundee
United, Jock became a fully fledged
professional player with Llanelli Town on
£12 a week but soon became homesick,
especially as he had left his wife and
young daughter behind and his home
had been broken into twice in his
absence. Celtic eventually stepped in
and paid £1,200 in 1951 for a player
that was initially seen as a reserve and
cover for the more established first
team players, but a succession of

injuries meant he got his chance at a
higher level. Appointed vice-captain
in 1952 he subsequently took over
as club captain from Sean Fallon when

RIGHT The 1955 team with Jock Stein third from left on the front row

Fallon broke his arm.

Whilst Fallon returned to the side and would score one of the goals that delivered a domestic double in 1954, Celtic's first since 1914 and the first time they had won the League since 1938, it was Jock Stein as captain that received the trophies. This was right, since it was Jock Stein's influence on and off the field that had turned Celtic's fortunes around. It was not to be to the last time either.

Persistent ankle injuries forced Jock to retire from playing in 1956 after 148 games for the club. He was appointed coach to the reserve and youth teams, and led the reserves to success in their cup competition in 1958, beating Rangers 8-2 on aggregate in the Final, his first success as a manager.

Keen to become a first team manager, Jock accepted an invitation to take over at Dunfermline Athletic in 1960 and steered them clear of relegation inside six weeks of arriving. The following year he took them to Scottish Cup victory, beating Celtic 2-0 in the Final after a replay. There then followed three years of European football before Jock moved on to Hibernian in April 1964, taking them to the Summer Cup within months of his arrival. It was a

temporary stay, however, for in March 1965 he returned to Celtic Park to take over a side that had not won the League or Scottish Cup since Jock's time as a player. All that was to change.

Just as he had done at Dunfermline and Hibernian, Jock introduced the Celtic players to novel training techniques, working with the ball, working on their skills, working out free kicks; anything that would give them an edge during a game. Inside six weeks Celtic had won the Scottish Cup, their first trophy of any kind since 1958 and the first of an astonishing 26 trophies he would win with the club.

The ten League titles, nine Scottish Cups and six League Cups are all overshadowed by the European Cup, won in 1967 in Celtic's debut season in the competition. It proved that Jock and his techniques, together with a special band of players he surrounded himself with, were more than a match for the rest of Europe. Whilst further European success proved elusive, with a runners-up spot in 1970 the closest they came, there was continued presence in European competition for the rest of the decade and beyond – Jock loved pitting his wits against foreign opposition.

A car crash in 1975 kept him away from the club for an entire season – Celtic finished empty handed. He returned and began building a side to once again challenge for honours, but to many he was a changed man. At the end of the 1977-78 season, another blank one for Celtic, Jock Stein agreed to step down as manager after thirteen glorious years in charge. He turned down an offer to run Celtic Pools, believing he still had something to offer the game and took over as manager of Leeds United, but after just 45 days he resigned to take over as Scotland manager, a position he had held on a part-time basis since 1965.

He took them to the 1982 World Cup Finals in Spain where they went out in the group stage on goal difference. They were on the brink of qualifying for the 1986 Finals in Mexico, requiring just a point in their final match against Wales, when Jock suffered a fatal heart attack, just after Scotland had equalised and got the point they needed. The circumstances might have seemed appropriate to some, but Celtic Park was not alone in mourning the greatest manager Scotland has ever seen.

Sutton

BORN IN NOTTINGHAM ON 10 March 1973, Chris Sutton began his career with Norwich City before earning a big money move to Blackburn Rovers in 1994. There he linked with Alan Shearer and helped them win the Premier League in 1995, their first title since 1914. Awarded a full cap for England in 1997 he seemed set to become a regular in the side but after a fall out with Glenn Hoddle over his refusal to turn out for the B side, he never featured again.

After Blackburn's relegation in 1999 he was sold to Chelsea for £10 million but struggled for his earlier form, prompting the club to sell him to Celtic for £6 million in the summer of 2000. At Celtic Park he linked with the likes of Henrik Larsson and John Hartson and would eventually help the club win three League titles, two Scottish Cups and two League Cups as well as reaching the Final of the UEFA Cup.

He was released on a free transfer in January 2006 and subsequently joined Birmingham City, although he struggled with injuries and made just eleven appearances for the club. When they were relegated from the Premier League at the end of the season, he was released.

BELOW Chris Sutton

Thomson

BORN IN KIRKCALDY IN 1909, John had all the attributes required to make a great goalkeeper – excellent handling ability, great positional sense and extreme bravery, the latter trait being indirectly responsible for his subsequent tragic death.

He played for Wellesley Juniors before joining Celtic in 1926 and made his debut the following year against Dundee, after a spell on loan at Ayr. He soon became a permanent fixture in the Celtic goal and, three years later, earned the first of his four caps for Scotland, proof of his growing stature within the game.

On 5 September 1931 John was in goal for the first meeting of the season between Rangers and Celtic at Ibrox. Five minutes into the second half, with the game still goalless, Rangers striker Sam English broke through the Celtic

defence and bore down on goal. John Thomson rushed out to meet him and dived at English's feet, just as the Rangers striker was about to shoot. Although John managed to block the shot, his momentum carried him onto English's knee, resulting in a sickening collision. Sam English managed to limp away from the incident, but John Thomson lay unconscious and in obvious need of urgent medical attention. Carried from the field with his head in bandages, he was rushed to hospital suffering from a depressed fracture of the skull and despite frantic surgery died later that evening from his injuries.

Twenty thousand lined the route for his funeral, his death provoking shock across Scottish football. Whilst a subsequent enquiry cleared Sam English of any blame, his career went into virtual decline thereafter, culminating in his early death. A memorial card printed for John Thomson revealed the depth of feeling towards the young Celtic goalkeeper – 'They never die who live in the hearts of those they leave behind.'

Tully

BORN IN BELFAST ON 11 JULY 1924, Charlie Tully began his career with Belfast Celtic and cost the Celtic Park club £8,000 when he was transferred in June 1948. What Celtic got for their money was a winger of supreme skill, able to seemingly win matches on his own when he was in the right mind but inconsistent at others.

For all his faults he was one of the club's first cult heroes, his performance against Rangers in a 3-1 Celtic victory seeing Tully mania hit the East End of Glasgow and Tully cocktails sold in pubs and bars, Tully ties in shops and even Tully green-coloured ice cream sold in cafes!

Charlie would win one League title, two Scottish Cups and two League Cups during his eleven years with Celtic, his inconsistency being matched in equal measure by his team-mates! He did, however, collect ten caps for Northern Ireland, scoring two goals directly from a corner in a 2-2 draw with England. It was a feat he repeated with Celtic against Falkirk – Charlie scored with one corner but the referee ordered the kick to be retaken, only to watch in bemusement as Charlie repeated the trick.

After a spell on loan with Stirling Albion he was released by Celtic in 1959 and had a spell as player manager of Cork Hibernians before managing Bangor twice and Portadown. He died in his sleep on 27 July 1971.

RIGHT Charlie Tully

Unbeaten

ON 13 NOVEMBER 1915 CELTIC were beaten at Tynecastle 2-0 by Hearts, only their third defeat in the League that season (although it was their third reverse in just four matches!). Celtic were not beaten again that season, winning 23 and drawing the other three of their matches as they won the League title by eleven points from Rangers.

They continued that form into the 1916-17 season, winning 26 and drawing ten as they went on to retain their League title, this time by ten points from Morton. On 21 April 1917, with the League title already won and Kilmarnock the visitors in the last home League match of the season, Celtic lost 2-0, thus ending a run of 62 matches without defeat. The run had produced 49 victories and 13 draws and represents the best ever run by the club since the formation of the Scottish League.

Celtic went through the entire 1897-98 season unbeaten, registering fifteen wins and three draws in their eighteen games and won the League by four points from Rangers. In more modern times Celtic lost their second League match of the 1967-68 season against Rangers, their only League defeat in the campaign as they won 30 and drew three of the 34 matches. The season also ended with Celtic crowned Champions, only two points ahead of Rangers who also lost only one match during the campaign.

Celtic have twice gone through a campaign losing once since the creation of the Scottish Premier League – in 1995-96, when they lost 2-0 to Rangers and ended runners-up in the League having drawn too many matches, and again in 2001-02, when Aberdeen won 2-0. Despite this, Celtic won the title in a canter, finishing eighteen points ahead of Rangers.

ABOVE Celtic fans show their support during the Scottish FA Cup Final match against Rangers, 1999

Viduka

BORN IN MELBOURNE ON
9 October 1975 of Croatian and
Ukranian descent, Mark Viduka
began his career in Australia with
Melbourne Croatia and made his
Australian debut in 1994. The following
year he moved to Croatia to play for
Croatia Zagreb, helping them into the
UEFA Cup during his three years with
the club.

A £3.5 million move brought him to
Celtic in December 1998 where he was
initially seen as a support to Henrik
Larsson and finished the campaign with
eight goals. The following season, which
saw Henrik Larsson out with a career-
threatening injury, Mark rose to the
challenge and rattled in 27 goals in all
competitions, helping them win the
League Cup and being named Player of
the Year by the PFA.

Despite this accolade, Mark claimed

he was only playing to 70% of his
capacity in Scotland, a comment that
did not particularly endear him to
either the fans or his team-mates. He
also had a tendency to play anony-
mously in the bigger matches, scoring
just one goal against Rangers in six
appearances. In the summer of 2000
therefore, new manager Martin O'Neill
sold him to Leeds United for £6 million
and used the money to bring in Chris
Sutton, a striker who would play to
100% of his capabilities.

Wallace

BORN IN KIRKINTILLOCH ON 23 June 1941, Willie Wallace began his career with Stenhousemuir in 1958 before moving on to Raith Rovers a year

later. There his performances earned him the nickname 'Wispy' as he would suddenly appear as if out of nowhere in the opponents' penalty area and score a vital goal. He earned his first call up for the Scottish League whilst with Raith Rovers and it wasn't long before bigger clubs came to take a look.

He was eventually sold to Hearts for £15,000 and would become top scorer for the club for four seasons, helping them win the League Cup in 1962-63. In December 1966 he was sold to Celtic (although he was apparently a boyhood Rangers fan!) for £30,000, where he was expected to form a partnership with Joe McBride in the Celtic front line. Injury to McBride meant Willie formed a new partnership with Stevie Chalmers, but it was a more than successful one, bringing the European Cup to Celtic Park at the end of his first season at the club.

In all he was to win five League titles, three Scottish Cups and two League Cups as well as four caps for Scotland (he won seven in total). He was still a member of the side that reached a second European Cup Final in 1970 and left the club for Crystal Palace in 1971, later playing for Dumbarton before emigrating to Australia.

World Club Championship

CELTIC'S REWARD FOR BEATING Internazionale in the European Cup Final in 1967 was a two-legged match against Racing Club of Buenos Aires in Argentina in the World Club Championship. The Championship had been introduced in 1960 but after an encouraging start, with Real Madrid beating Penarol 5-1 on aggregate, had developed into virtual all out war between the two competing sides. Celtic versus Racing Club would be no different.

The Argentinian side were visitors to Glasgow for the first leg, a match that was switched to Hampden Park in order to accommodate all of those who wished to attend, including British Prime Minister Harold Wilson. A crowd of 103,000 was present to see Celtic win 1-0 thanks to a goal from Billy McNeill, but that goal was a brief respite from some quite disgraceful scenes on the night. Racing Club had come intent on keeping the score as low as possible, kicking, spitting, punching and

employing any tactic to unsettle the Celtic players. Jock Stein was more than bemused by the Racing Club tactics, he was almost fearful for his players when they journeyed to Argentina for the second leg.

The flight was greeted with a warm reception when it touched down at Buenos Aires, with flowers and gifts being presented to the players. It turned distinctly chilly the following night and the hostilities began even before the match kicked off. Ronnie Simpson was felled by a missile many Celtic players were convinced was thrown by a photographer, with the resulting gash forcing him out of the side and John Fallon called up as his replacement. Tommy Gemmell gave Celtic the lead from the penalty spot but Racing eventually scored twice to take the tie into a third, decisive play-off in Montevideo a few days later.

Celtic were determined to win this match, as much for their own reputation as anything else, but once again were not helped by coming up against a side that was more concerned with stopping them at all costs. Jimmy Johnstone had come in for some harsh tackling and treatment in the two

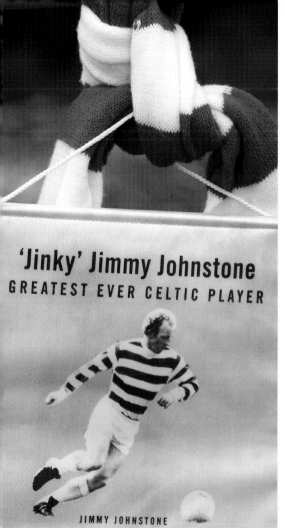

'Jinky' Jimmy Johnstone
GREATEST EVER CELTIC PLAYER

JIMMY JOHNSTONE

previous matches and this was to be no different, and when he was hacked down by Rulli a number of players from both sides became involved in a scuffle on the pitch. Police armed with batons rather than the referee eventually restored order, but the referee decided to send off Basile of Racing Club and Celtic's Bobby Lennox, even though Lennox had not been involved!

If the dismissals were intended to calm things down it did not have the desired effect. Jimmy Johnstone retaliated after being kicked once too often and was sent off shortly before Racing Club scored the only goal of the game. Near the end John Hughes was sent off for aiming a kick at the Racing goalkeeper, soon to be joined by Racing's

LEFT Jimmy Johnstone who had been part of a grudge match between Racing Club and Celtic

Rulli who finally got his just desserts after he had punched John Clark, another incident that required police intervention. There was still time for Bertie Auld to become the fourth Celtic player to be ordered off, but he refused to leave the field and the referee eventually blew for time.

Although they had been on the receiving end of just about every trick imaginable, the Celtic players were not to escape further punishment, but this time it was dished out by their own club. Chairman Robert Kelly announced five days later 'We are in this together, from the chairman to the players. We feel that for our reputation and also for the reputation of football, the players must suffer for their conduct. We do not want to individualise and we are taking the unprecedented step of fining the whole team £250 per player.'

RIGHT Snowmen wearing Rangers and Celtic strips

Xmas Day

WHILST FOOTBALL MATCHES played on Christmas Day were taken as part and parcel of the festivities in England for many a year, with the last of these being played in 1958, in Scotland these were only played if Christmas Day fell on a Saturday, and then only as part of the normal fixture list. Thus Christmas Day matches continued in Scotland for some 13 years after they had been halted in England. Here therefore is a list of League matches played by Celtic on Christmas Day.

Year	Opponents	Venue	Score
1897	Clyde	Away	9-1
1909	Kilmarnock	Away	1-0
1915	Airdrie	Home	6-0
1920	St Mirren	Away	2-0
1926	Kilmarnock	Home	6-0
1933	Queens Park	Away	3-2
1934	Queens Park	Home	4-1
1937	Kilmarnock	Home	8-0
1946	Queens Park	Home	1-0
1947	Hearts	Home	4-2
1948	Aberdeen	Home	3-0
1954	Clyde	Away	2-2
1957	Queen Of The South	Home	1-2
1965	Morton	Home	8-1
1971	Hearts	Home	3-2

Young

BORN IN KILMARNOCK, HALF-BACK Jim Young joined Celtic from Bristol Rovers in 1903 having plied his trade in the Southern League. That Celtic were able to sign him on a free transfer made his value to the side even more remarkable, for what was Bristol Rovers' loss was undoubtedly Celtic's gain.

He stepped straight into the side for the match against Partick Thistle in August 1903 and would go on to make 443 first team appearances, scoring fourteen goals. If his own goalscoring prowess wasn't that great it was entirely down to the role he was expected to play for the team – providing the link between defence and attack and often being the starting point for many a move that led to a goal. It was his promptings that enabled Celtic to win nine League titles and five Scottish Cups during his time with the club, although

Jim was unfortunate to have won only one cap for Scotland during his career, this coming against Ireland in 1906.

Despite the success, Jim always looked as though he had a scowl on his face, leading him to be nicknamed 'Sunny Jim Young'. A knee injury sustained in the autumn of 1916 meant he missed the rest of the season, although Celtic managed to complete their fourth consecutive title at the end of the campaign. Jim retired at the end of the season at the age of 35 and was a huge loss to the club – they won only one title out of the next four.

Zurawski

BORN IN POZNAN, POLAND ON 12 September 1976, Maciej Zurawski proved to be a useful acquisition for Celtic when he joined in July 2005, helping the club win the League Cup and League title at the end of his first season.

He joined the club from Wisla Krakow, where he established a reputation for being technically gifted with a thunderbolt shot and a keen eye for goal. He was already an established member of the Poland team at the time he moved to Celtic and has since gone on to add to his tally of caps for his country.

His performances for Celtic were eye catching, culminating in a four goal blast that helped Celtic beat Dunfermline 6-1 and establish a new Premier goalscoring record in February 2006, a result even more remarkable as it was achieved away from home! It helped 'Magic', as he is known by Celtic fans, collect the Player of the Month award for February, recognition at last for a player many feel had been underrated. Generally considered one of the best Celtic players of their title-winning season, greater things are anticipated for Magic in the future.

LEFT Maciej Zurawski (R) is handed the Bank of Scotland Premier League trophy by team mate John Hartson following the 1-1 draw with Hibernian, April 2006.

Available Now

Available from all major stockists of books or online at:
www.greenumbrellashop.co.uk

The pictures in this book were provided courtesy of

GETTY IMAGES
www.gettyimages.com

EMPICS
www.empics.com

Design and artwork by Jane Stephens

Image research by Ellie Charleston

Published by Green Umbrella Publishing

Series Editors Jules Gammond, Vanessa Gardner

Written by Graham Betts